AF166697

CAMBRIDGE LIBRARY COLLECTION

Books of enduring scholarly value

Music

The systematic academic study of music gave rise to works of description, analysis and criticism, by composers and performers, philosophers and anthropologists, historians and teachers, and by a new kind of scholar - the musicologist. This series makes available a range of significant works encompassing all aspects of the developing discipline.

Wagner and His Isolde

The German poet Mathilde Wesendonck (1828–1902), author of the texts of the *Wesendonck Lieder*, was the wife of Wagner's patron, the wealthy silk merchant Otto Wesendonck. From 1852 until 1858, the Wagners lived next to the Wesendoncks in Zurich and an intense relationship developed between Wagner and Mathilde, subsequently reflected in the impossible love at the heart of his opera *Tristan und Isolde*. Prepared by the American musicologist Gustav Kobbé (1857–1918), who provides a helpful connecting narrative, this 1905 translation of a selection of 'the most intimate and striking' of Wagner's impassioned letters to Mathilde charts the course of the opera's creation. Written between 1853 and 1863, the letters show Wagner thinking aloud not only about *Tristan* but also the planning of *Parsifal*. As Mathilde's letters to Wagner were destroyed, the exact nature of their relationship and of her inspiration musically will never be fully established.

Cambridge University Press has long been a pioneer in the reissuing of out-of-print titles from its own backlist, producing digital reprints of books that are still sought after by scholars and students but could not be reprinted economically using traditional technology. The Cambridge Library Collection extends this activity to a wider range of books which are still of importance to researchers and professionals, either for the source material they contain, or as landmarks in the history of their academic discipline.

Drawing from the world-renowned collections in the Cambridge University Library and other partner libraries, and guided by the advice of experts in each subject area, Cambridge University Press is using state-of-the-art scanning machines in its own Printing House to capture the content of each book selected for inclusion. The files are processed to give a consistently clear, crisp image, and the books finished to the high quality standard for which the Press is recognised around the world. The latest print-on-demand technology ensures that the books will remain available indefinitely, and that orders for single or multiple copies can quickly be supplied.

The Cambridge Library Collection brings back to life books of enduring scholarly value (including out-of-copyright works originally issued by other publishers) across a wide range of disciplines in the humanities and social sciences and in science and technology.

Wagner and His Isolde

GUSTAV KOBBÉ

CAMBRIDGE
UNIVERSITY PRESS

CAMBRIDGE
UNIVERSITY PRESS

University Printing House, Cambridge, CB2 8BS, United Kingdom

Cambridge University Press is part of the University of Cambridge.

It furthers the University's mission by disseminating knowledge in the pursuit of
education, learning and research at the highest international levels of excellence.

www.cambridge.org
Information on this title: www.cambridge.org/9781108078559

© in this compilation Cambridge University Press 2015

This edition first published 1905
This digitally printed version 2015

ISBN 978-1-108-07855-9 Paperback

This book reproduces the text of the original edition. The content and language reflect
the beliefs, practices and terminology of their time, and have not been updated.

Cambridge University Press wishes to make clear that the book, unless originally published
by Cambridge, is not being republished by, in association or collaboration with,
or with the endorsement or approval of, the original publisher or its successors in title.

WAGNER AND HIS ISOLDE

MATHILDE WESENDONK
(1860)
After a Painting by C. Dorner

WAGNER
AND HIS ISOLDE

BY

GUSTAV KOBBÉ

Author of " Wagner's Music Dramas Analysed,"
" Loves of the Great Composers," "Opera
Singers," "Signora," etc.

Illustrations

NEW YORK
DODD, MEAD & COMPANY
1905

COPYRIGHT, 1905,
BY
DODD, MEAD & COMPANY

Published September, 1905

To

HERMAN BEHR

*Whose discernment and enthusiasm were a
guide and an inspiration to me while
writing this book*

AUTHOR'S NOTE

On reading, in the German original, the letters and journals relating to one of the most fascinating episodes in Wagner's career, his romance with Mathilde Wesendonk, who inspired his " Tristan und Isolde," it seemed to me a foregone conclusion that the book would be translated in its entirety. But as a complete translation could result only in a bulky and somewhat expensive publication, and as, in my judgment, there were many portions which could be omitted without lessening its interest for English readers, it appeared feasible to take the most intimate and striking passages as a basis for a smaller volume. This I have done; and I trust that, with the introduction and the connecting narrative which I have supplied, the story of Wagner and his Isolde has been told without any serious omissions.

I have had the good fortune to obtain from a New Yorker, who knew Mathilde Wesendonk well, some delightful personal impressions of her, as well as the quaint and charming photographs of herself and her husband taken in Rome in 1861.

This book was written, set up and cast before the complete translation by Mr. Ellis was published.

GUSTAV KOBBÉ.

CONTENTS

I

"TRISTAN UND ISOLDE" IN REAL LIFE

CONTENTS

II

A LONELY EXILE IN VENICE

CONTENTS

III

THE MOAN OF A BREAKING HEART

xi

CONTENTS

IV

AN INTERMEZZO AT LUCERNE

V

VICISSITUDES IN PARIS

CONTENTS

CONTENTS

VI

SUCH STUFF AS DREAMS ARE MADE OF

ILLUSTRATIONS

"TRISTAN UND ISOLDE" IN REAL LIFE

I

THE spell of romance long has linked the names of Richard Wagner and Mathilde Wesendonk, but it has been a spell woven by hearsay rather than by certain evidence. Hints have been found in his correspondence that she was the good angel of at least part of his exile in Switzerland, but the full story of the place this lovely woman occupied in his heart, and the influence she exerted over him and his art, still remained to be told.

At last, however, the world has been taken into the confidence of the great musical and dramatic genius, and into that of the woman who inspired his most impassioned creation, his " Tristan und Isolde." Now that she is dead, the letters he wrote to her have been published—letters in which passionate longing alternate with supreme effort at resignation, and in which he more than once invokes blessings upon her as the inspiration of his Isolde. These letters Wagner himself wished to have destroyed. Mathilde, however, well divining their importance to posterity, piously preserved them, and in her latter years ordered and arranged them for publication, so that in due time they might be given to the world.

THE GREATEST PSYCHOLOGICAL ROMANCE IN MUSIC

How irretrievable would have been the loss had she observed Wagner's wish and destroyed them! What insight they give us into the character of the great poet-dramatist and composer! Nothing he has written about himself, nothing others have written about him, show him in a light at once so clear and so fine. They are worth the whole vast volume of Wagner literature up to date. They take us into his inner consciousness, disclose his heart to us, make us at home in his very soul. Moreover, they form the greatest psychological romance in the history of modern music. "Tristan und Isolde" first was performed on the stage at Munich in 1865; but long before that it was played in real life at Zurich, and with the following cast:

4

"TRISTAN" IN REAL LIFE

Tristan	*Richard Wagner*
Isolde	*Mathilde Wesendonk*
King Mark	*Otto Wesendonk*
Brangäne	*Frau Wille*
Kurwenal	*Jacob Sulzer*
Melot	*Everybody*

The shepherd, the sailors were missing, but their places, like Melot's, may be said to have been taken by the gossips of Zurich. In every affair of the heart there are gossips—especially if the parties to it are the husband and wife of somebody else.

THE HEROINE OF A PASSION

If these letters are a monument to Wagner, they also are a monument to Mathilde and Otto Wesendonk. In this great heart-crisis of her life Mathilde became the heroine of a passion, but she did not allow herself to become the victim of a liaison. I believe Otto Wesendonk deserves some, possible much, of the credit for this. He retained Mathilde's confidence, and at the psychical moment managed the affair with a combination of tact and determination which sent Wagner off to a second exile in Venice, while she remained, faithful to her duties as wife and mother, in

5

Zurich. At the same time he was high-minded enough not to break with Wagner; and appreciating that it is the privilege of genius to arrogate to itself more than a common mortal may dare aspire to, he remained the composer's friend, and on several occasions thereafter came to his aid, as he had before, in sore financial straits. Whoever reads "Tristan und Isolde" aright as a drama, not of consummation, but of renunciation, will realise that while Otto was the King Mark of the Zurich episode, there was this difference—he stayed at home instead of going hunting.

WHO WAS MATHILDE?

Mathilde was born December 23, 1828, in Elberfeld. She was educated partly in Dusseldorf, whither her parents had removed, partly at boarding school. Her father was Karl Luckemeyer, a wholesale dry-goods merchant. On May 19, 1848, she was married to Otto Wesendonk, who was a partner of the New York silk importing house of Loesching, Wesendonk & Co., and its foreign representative. Later the firm became Kutter, Luckemeyer & Co., so that both her own family and that of her husband have had rep-

resentatives in New York. In fact, the business of the firm still is carried on by successors, and children of Otto Wesendonk's
brother Hugo still reside in New York.

A FAMOUS GOLD PEN

In 1850, before they met Wagner, Otto and
Mathilde came to America, remaining most
of the time in New York, where they were
widely entertained, both for their own agreeable qualities and because of the prominence
of the Wesendonk family in that city. In
connection with the Wesendonks' visit to
America it is interesting to note that an
American product was to stand in close relationship to several of Wagner's greatest
compositions. For after he met the Wesendonks, Mathilde presented him with an American gold pen, with which, as he himself writes
to Liszt, he wrote the score of " Die Walküre," characterising it as a model of the cali-
graphic art. But this was not the only time
the pen was called into requisition. In a
letter written to Mathilde from Venice, Wagner mentions " the same pen " as being used
by him on the " Tristan " score; and in a
letter to Wesendonk in 1870 (sixteen years

after the pen had been presented to him), he states that he wrote the "Meistersinger" score with it. While the only direct references Wagner makes to this pen are in connection with the "Walküre," "Tristan" and "Meistersinger" scores, it is not unreasonable to suppose that "Siegfried," "Götterdämmerung," and even "Parsifal," may have been written with it. But even without these this American gold pen still would have a remarkable record.

MATHILDE AS A FRIEND RECALLS HER

It gives added interest to the romantic story of Wagner and Mathilde from the American point of view to realise that the woman who inspired Isolde once was here, and that there are in New York people who knew her and remember her. "Mathilde," said one of her American friends to me, "was a woman of refined and poetic beauty; slender and graceful and with a lovely winning smile, the kind of woman who exercises a charm over every circle she enters." My informant not only knew Mathilde and her husband in New York, he continued on terms of intimacy with

them, visiting them in Zurich in the very villa
which the Wagner episode has made famous,
and subsequently in their residences in Dresden and Berlin, and at their country seat on
the Traunsee in the Austrian Tyrol.

"Otto Wesendonk," he says, "was one of the
few men who, having been active in business
until he was forty-five years old, was able to
retire, display a lively interest in all branches
of art, and yet retain sufficient business
acumen to make investments which invariably
turned out well." The air of distinction
which my informant found in their home, he
believes to have been due to Otto as well as to
Mathilde, though more, it is true, to the latter
than to the former.

ARISTOCRATIC, ETHEREAL, FAIRY-LIKE

Mathilde he characterises as aristocratic,
ethereal, fairy-like, and with highly ideal
views of life and art—"always in the air,"
as he expresses it. In Berlin her aristocratic
appearance caused her to be known as the
"Princess." She went out little herself, but
distinguished people flocked to her house—
diplomats, artists, musicians, scientists.
When her daughter Myrrha, who had been

9

married to Freiherr von Bissing, died, three empresses sent flowers for her bier—Augusta, widow of William I, Empress Frederick, and the present Empress. My informant literally became a " house guest " at the Wesendonk villa in Zurich, where he attended the University. This was a little less than two years after Wagner had left Zurich. In 1860 the Wesendonks made a trip to Rome. While there they had their photographs taken. These, with the place and year of sitting inscribed in her handwriting, Mathilde presented to my friend, through whose courtesy I have been able to use them, as well as the photograph of Myrrha, here.

MATHILDE INTERCEDES

Student-like, my friend was apt to " cut " such lectures as did not particularly interest him, and Otto, as a sort of unofficial guardian, sometimes took him to task for this, on which occasions Mathilde graciously would put in a good word for him. He was, however, extremely interested in art and regularly attended the lectures delivered by Lübke, the famous author of the " History of Art." One time when he was at the Wes-

endonk villa, the young student was introduced to the famous professor, who turned
to Wesendonk and said, "I know this young
man well by sight. He always occupies one
of the front seats at my lectures." Mathilde
could not conceal her pleasure that for once
her husband had no chance to take my friend
to task for neglecting his studies.

I have said above that during the whole
Wagner episode Mathilde retained her husband's confidence. Not only is this confirmed, as I shall point out later, by passages
in the correspondence, but my informant
states that, when Wagner began to interest
her deeply, and her husband became uneasy,
she told the latter that she always would be
faithful to her duties as a wife and a mother,
but that "Wagner had opened to her a horizon such as no one else could."

The composer found her a placid, happy,
graceful creature. He left her with her
nature vibrant, uplifted, tuned to harmony
with the infinite; an æolian harp, sensitive to
the most delicate breath of feeling.

TENDER MEMORIES

She herself says that when she met Wagner

in 1852 at the house of Dresden friends who
were living in Zurich, the family of the law-
yer, Hermann Marschall von Bieberstein, she
was as simple and untutored as a blank page.
It was quite characteristic of the composer
that he could not see a blank page without
wanting to write on it, and in his own way.
Before he left Zurich, in 1858, he had written " Wagner " all over this one.

It was not until about a year after his
meeting with Mathilde that the intercourse
between the composer and her family became
more intimate. Wagner had been wonderfully attracted by her, and, finding the
" blank page " receptive to his ideas and
ambitions, he began to take her into his confidence regarding the great works which he
had planned. At that time he was largely
engaged in literary work, and having completed the " Nibelung " dramas, he delighted her by reading them to her, and after
that she saw everything he wrote before it
was submitted to anyone else. He himself
was an ardent admirer of Beethoven, and
finding that she, too, was deeply interested
in the composer, he would play over the
sonatas for her; or if he had a concert to

conduct in which a Beethoven symphony was on the programme, he would analyse it for her beforehand, until she became as enthusiastic over the work as he himself.

" BLESSED BE MATHILDE! "

In 1854 he sent her the first composition sketches of the " Walküre." After the Vorspiel he wrote the letters " G. S. M.," which stand for G(esegnet) S(ei) M(athilde) (Blessed be Mathilde)!—Verily the page was blank no longer.

In January of the following year he rewrote his " Faust " overture which he had composed in Paris in 1840. He had intended to dedicate it to her, but it suddenly occurred to him that the motto quoted from Goethe's drama which he had placed above the score was too terribly gloomy, so he contented himself with presenting her with the original score, under which he wrote: " R. W., Zurich, 17 January, 1855, a souvenir for a dear woman."

HER " DUSK MAN "

Mathilde also notes down memories of a trip to Brunnen, where at dusk he would play

13

passages from the "Eroica" and the C Minor symphonies, while in the morning he would awaken her with selections from "Lohengrin." When he became deeply impressed with the philosophy of Schopenhauer he explained that philosopher's theories to her, and, in fact, always was careful to draw her attention to every new light in literature and science, reading the books or communicating their contents to her. When after this prolonged purely literary activity he again began to compose, it was his custom to visit her toward evening and play for her what he had written that day. Usually it was the hour between five and six o'clock, which led him to dub himself the "dusk man."

STORY OF THE WALHALLA MOTIVE

Occasionally his own musical setting of some phrase would not suit him, and after playing it for her he would seek then and there to obtain a better version. This was the case with the Walhalla motive in "Rheingold."

"Master, let it stand as it is," she said.

14

"No, no, I can improve it," he protested. He paced the salon awhile, then abruptly left her. The following afternoon he did not appear, and also absented himself the second and third day. On the fourth he stole in and, seating himself at the piano without a word, played the motive unchanged—just as it had been the first day.

"Well?" she asked.

"Yes, yes," he said, "you were right. It cannot be improved." A verdict in which posterity agrees with him.

Mathilde says that he gave an added stimulus to every circle he entered. If he came into the room weary and unnerved by work, it was beautiful to behold how, after a short rest and distraction, the clouds lifted from his face and a light passed over his features, especially when he seated himself at the piano.

FIVE PIANOS AND A FLUTE!

His lodgings in one of the faubourgs of Zurich were roomy and comfortable, but the piano playing which went on about him was a nuisance to him, especially when he composed. (He himself mentions five pianos and a flute going simultaneously.)

Mathilde tells us that there was a smithy opposite, and that, when he was composing the Forging of the Sword in " Siegfried," he made an arrangement with the smith not to hammer in the morning. It was Wagner's longing for a quiet spot where he could work undisturbed which led Mathilde to offer him through her husband a châlet on the grounds of the beautiful villa which Otto Wesendonk built on the Green Hill.

" Money affairs," according to Mathilde, " he hated with his whole soul. In his intercourse with me during countless beautiful and consecrated hours, they never were referred to."

Her life of ease and luxury Wagner turned into a joke when one morning she appeared at a concert rehearsal. " The very stones are astonished," he exclaimed, " to see Frau Wesendonk in the streets at ten o'clock."

His intercourse with Otto was most agreeable. When he received a diploma of honorary membership in the Dutch Musical Society, for which he did not care a snap, he sent it to Wesendonk with the admonition, " Hang it up in your office " ; humorously adding, " It may give you new strength and courage."

16

On the whole, however, there can be little doubt that Mathilde was intellectually and spiritually above her husband, something which is amusingly shown in a casual sentence of Wagner's friend, the author, Gottfried Keller, who speaks of " Frau Wesendonk and her husband and children " as being at a certain function, instead of saying " Herr Wesendonk and his family."

ENTER WAGNER

The above will have given some idea of who Mathilde was and of the influence which Wagner exerted upon her. But who was Wagner at this period of his career? He was thirty-nine years old, and so far as the opinion of the world was concerned, a failure—but a failure with enormous confidence in his ultimate success. Except, however, for a very small circle of the elect, most prominent among them Liszt, people who paused long enough to think of him at all thought of him as a fit subject for a musical lunatic asylum. His means were scant. Had it not been for an annual stipend allowed him by Mme. Julie Ritter, a Dresden admirer, and for money sent to him by Liszt, he would have been obliged to live by absolute drudgery.

A POLITICAL REFUGEE

Owing to his participation in the Revolution of 1849, he had been forced to flee from Dresden, where he was a conductor at the Opera. Stopping over at Weimar with Liszt, he learned that a police circular giving a description of him had been issued and that the authorities were on his track. With money which Liszt hastily managed to borrow from his *amie*, the Princess Carolyne Sayn-Wittgenstein, Wagner contrived to flee to Zurich. Later he was joined there by his wife, the money for her travelling expenses again being furnished by his fidus Achates, Liszt.

HIS WIFE UNAPPRECIATIVE

Wagner's wife was Minna Plane, of Magdeburg, whom he had married in 1836 at Königsberg, where he conducted the Opera. She was an actress, without, however, any excess of temperament, and far beneath him intellectually. Accounts seem to agree that she possessed personal attractions, but the life she had led with Wagner had been one of almost continual pecuniary difficulties and privations, and she had aged rapidly. Undoubtedly she was an admirable helpmeet in the household. Wagner himself acknowledged that she would have made an excellent wife for a commonplace man; but she utterly failed to appreciate his genius. He was an eagle, she a ground sparrow. Of his four operas, "Rienzi," "The Flying Dutchman," "Tannhäuser," and "Lohengrin," only "Rienzi" was comprehensible to her. It had been a success and brought in money. She could not understand why he had abandoned this brilliant style of composition for schemes like his vast "Nibelung" dramas, which to her seemed chimerical. She, too, was a "blank page," but, unlike Mathilde, a blank page which did not inspire in Wagner a desire to exercise his chirography. It only required the appearance of an Isolde upon the scene to turn this difference into a tragedy and— Isolde appeared.

LONGING FOR WOMANLY SYMPATHY

Wagner's letters to Liszt show how much he longed for womanly sympathy, a sympathy which his wife did not give him. "Let

19

us look upon the world through the medium
of contempt alone; only the heart of a friend,
the tears of a woman, can dispel its curse."
And to another friend (Uhlig) he writes that
he could be inspired with new hope by the
" moist gleaming of a woman's eyes."

It is significant that he penned these sen-
tences after he had met Mathilde, the woman
who was to become the author of the " Five
Poems " which he set to music, and which included the famous " Dreams," the germ of
the great love duet in the second act of
" Tristan." When " Dreams " was written
by her and composed by him, time already had
sufficed for the relation between this extraordinary man and this lovely woman to ripen
from friendship to a companionship, which
in turn was to become a sympathetic union
of souls, a psychological romance which was
to find its consummation in that outpouring
of genius known to the world as " Tristan
und Isolde," but really the story of Wagner
and Mathilde.

I already have intimated that when Wagner
and Mathilde met his means were sparse.
The generosity of Frau Julie Ritter and
Liszt's unflagging interest, which led him to

respond as best he could to his friend's many appeals for aid, should be placed to the everlasting credit. There were royalties from the performances of Wagner's works, but they hardly would have sufficed for sustenance. He lived in quarters which were luxurious for his means, but doubtless he felt that his great plans, which could not materialise for many years, justified him in calling on his friends for aid. However indifferent the world at large remained to him, everyone who came in contact with him seemed impressed with his genius. Thus his landlady, Frau Stockar-Escher, who was clever with her brush, painted a portrait of him, which has several times been reproduced and is considered one of the best portraits of him at that period of his life.

THE FIRST LETTER

But the admiration of a few of the elect could not save him from moments of deep depression. His " Lohengrin " produced by Liszt at Weimar still remained a mute score to him, and as a matter of fact, on account of his exile, it was not until thirteen years after he had composed it that he heard it performed. His correspondence shows that he appreciated how far in advance of the time his " Nibelung " dramas were, and that often he despaired of ever producing them during his lifetime. Little wonder if on occasion he felt that the world was against him, and that he gave way to his moods.

APOLOGIES TO MATHILDE

Apparently, even the Wesendonks were not spared such outbursts, for the very first letter which he wrote to Mathilde, and which is dated Zurich, March 17, 1853, is an apology to her for his behaviour on the previous evening.

" Heaven protect you from any further rudeness of mine," he writes; " for now you must realise that it was no mere empty caprice, if often my acceptance of your friendly invitations were coupled with the dread that my moodiness would make martyrs of those who wished me well, in the same degree as it tortures me. If hereafter I deny myself the pleasure of this social intercourse —and after occurrences like yesterday's, should I not?—be assured that I do so only in the hope of earning your forgiveness by appearing before you in a more favourable light.

" I hope to hear to-morrow from your husband in Basle, that your equanimity, which means so much to me, has not been more than temporarily disturbed by my ill-natured talk. With this heartfelt wish I commend myself to your merciful forbearance."

The early letters are comparatively brief. Indeed, the bulk of the correspondence dates after Wagner's departure from Zurich— after events had made it impossible for him to retain his intimate footing in the Wesendonk household.

Wesendonk was active in guaranteeing the expenses of three concerts which Wagner gave in May, 1853. This and the events themselves which offered Mathilde an opportunity of hearing Wagner's music under his own direction, a circumstance which was likely to give added stimulus to her growing appreciation of his genius, doubtless drew them closer together. At all events, a billet dispatched to her by Wagner on June 1 of the same year is significant because of the somewhat exaggerated expression with which it closes. He asks Mathilde to come to his lodgings in the evening (probably for music) and adds: " I shall ask no one else, in order that nothing may mar the sanctity of this evening."

"KNOWEST THOU HOW 'TWILL BE?"

Besides the guarantee for the concerts, Wesendonk during June advanced money to Wagner. It was in recognition of this that Wagner composed the short "Album Sonata," which he sent to Mathilde, and on which he wrote as a motto, "Wisst ihr wie das wirt?" (Knowest thou how 'twill be?), the Norns' question in "Götterdämmerung," and accompanied in the score by the motive of Fate, a circumstance which may well be emphasised here. For fate was beginning to interweave the strands of these two lives.

One cannot well imagine Wagner a composer of light dance music, but this mention of the "Album Sonata" reminds me that, when Mathilde's sister Marie was visiting her in Zurich, he dashed off a trifle which he sent to her under the title of "Zuricher Vielliebchen Walzer or Polka or anything else, written by the best dancer from Saxony." Wagner's genius occasionally found an outlet in humorous sallies of this sort.

In the letter accompanying the sonata Wag-

ner says that it is the first thing he has
composed in six years, which was a slight ex-
aggeration. It was the first thing composed
by him in five years, which was quite bad
enough. He had been busy with the poems of
his "Nibelung" dramas and other literary
work. Later, during this same summer, he
applied to Wesendonk for another loan in
order that he might, through a change of
scene and air, be stimulated to take up composition again. Needless to say, this generous
friend complied with the request, and in August Wagner started for Italy. In three
weeks he was back again in Zurich. The trip
was to have lasted much longer, but Wagner's
health did not seem to benefit by the change.
So he came home. Or was Mathilde the mag-
net that drew him back? Sunny Italy?—The
skies of Zurich with Mathilde were brighter!

THE WEAVING OF THE STRANDS

Short as it was, however, the trip had the
desired musical result. Wagner himself reported (in a letter to Boito) that the opening music of "Das Rheingold" came to him
during a sleepless night in an inn at Spezzia.
Thus the Wesendonks were instrumental in

stimulating Wagner's musical genius to take
up the composition of the " Ring." It does
not require a great stretch of the imagination to believe that Mathilde was not without
influence in persuading Otto to make the loan
which enabled Wagner to undertake the trip
that had the beginning of work on the " Nibelung" music as its result. Indeed, the inter-
twining of the strands in the lives of this
inspired man and this spiritual woman became
closer and closer as their friendship pro-
gressed. Unconsciously at first, perhaps, she
grew to be the partner of his thoughts. He
initiated her into his ideas, his plans. His
inspiration was, so to speak, dissected for her
in advance by himself. What the famous gold
pen was to write she knew beforehand. What
it wrote she was the first to see. And what an
inspiration it is to know that a loving woman
is waiting eagerly for what you have written!

BRUNNHILDE SLEEPS

Even the first pencilled composition sketches
of the " Ring " were presented to Mathilde
by the composer. She knew how to value
them. Carefully, line by line, dot by dot, she
went over them in ink, then had a small red

portfolio made in which she treasured these rare mementos of the workings of a great mind. Besides their incalculable value as such, they hold the mirror up to the past, for Wagner noted on them the precise dates of composition: "Rheingold," 1st November, 1853, to 14th January, 1854; "Walküre," Act I, 1st June to September, 1854; Act II, September to November, 1854; Act III, 20th November to 27th December, 1854; "Siegfried," Act I, finished January, 1857; Act II, 22d May to 30th July, 1857.

These sketches, up to and including the second act of "Siegfried," were completely worked out while Wagner still was in Zurich. But the third act of "Siegfried" was only sketched. For here the composition of the "Nibelung" dramas was broken off. Siegfried and Brünnhilde were thrust aside for Tristan and Isolde.

"Brünnhilde sleeps," wrote Wagner to Liszt. He might have added, "Isolde awakens."

MOTIVE OF SYMPATHY

More, however, remains to be said regarding Mathilde's relation to the "Nibelung"

27

dramas. "Come over for the last act of 'Die Walküre,'" Wagner writes; and at the end of another epistle, which, like the one I have just quoted from, is undated, he places the Motive of Sympathy from the "Die Walküre," and significantly adds a question mark.

Note the meaning! The Motive of Sympathy! This is the brief phrase which in "Die Walküre" wells up from the orchestra as spontaneously as pity mingled with sympathetic sorrow wells up from the heart of a gentle woman. Bear in mind the action which it accompanies. The storm-driven Siegmund has entered Hunding's dwelling to seek shelter there. The door to the left has opened, and Sieglinde has appeared. Hearing someone enter, and thinking her husband has returned, she has come into the hall to meet him. In his stead an exhausted stranger has thrown himself on the bearskin rug near the hearth. She approaches and bends compassionately over him. What was Wagner hint-

28

ing at? This compassionate action is accompanied by the Motive of Sympathy which here is heard for the first time. Some commentators have called it the Motive of Compassion, but I have preferred Sympathy as expressing that subtle tie between two souls which at first is invisible, even to those whom it unites. At the time Siegmund and Sieglinde are strangers to each other. Yet as the woman bends over the hunted, storm-beaten fugitive it is that subtle sympathy which causes her to regard him with more tenderness than she would bestow upon any other unfortunate stranger. Her compassion, her sympathy, are joined to a prescience which she herself cannot explain.

Let me call attention to another passage in " Die Walküre," where this same motive accompanies the action, and to the " business " of the episode. " She slowly raises her eyes to his " are the stage directions. " Both gaze long and silently at each other with an expression of intense emotion."

What was Wagner hinting at, even before " Tristan und Isolde " had taken shape in his mind, when he sent the Motive of Sympathy to Mathilde? For what is this motive in the drama but the earliest premonition of that love between Siegmund and Sieglinde which sent them forth in ecstatic flight into the Spring night?

"I AM IN TROUBLE AT HOME"

There is another undated note to Mathilde. "My wife who is busy in the kitchen," begins Wagner. "My wife who is busy in the kitchen!" We may be sure Mathilde never was busy in the kitchen. We may be equally sure that the Motive of Sympathy was not shown to Minna. Poor meagre soul—she was busy in the kitchen! One wonders what Wagner would have done if she had not been. Possibly he would have dined at the Wesendonks.

"I am in trouble at home," he writes to Mathilde on another occasion, "because you spoke disrespectfully of 'Rienzi'!" But after all was not "Rienzi" preferable to the "Die Walküre" from Minna's point of view? There was no Motive of Sympathy in it.

"WHAT WOULD 'TANTE' SAY?"

Part of 1855 Wagner spent in London, as conductor of the Philharmonic concerts. From

London he wrote Wesendonk an amusing letter on the British passion for oratorio. " For hours they sit there and listen to one fugue after another, convinced that they are doing something commendable, for which they will be rewarded by going to a heaven where all the music consists of Italian operatic airs. Mendelssohn well understood how to take advantage of this pious impulse of the British public, and composed and conducted oratorios for its benefit, and therefore has become the real Messiah of the English musical world.

" What would ' Tante ' say if I were to compose an oratorio for Exeter Hall? "

This joke about his composing an oratorio for Exeter Hall is quite as amusing as, in the light of subsequent events, his allusion to his future Isolde as " Tante." Aunt Isolde forsooth!

MOURNS FOR HIS FAITHFUL DOG

When Wagner returned to Zurich in July, 1855, a sorrow awaited him. He was a passionate lover of animals, and especially of dogs. He had a dog, " Peps," to which he was so deeply attached that Liszt desiring to express his own friendship for the composer once dubbed himself "Double Peps" and "Double extract of Peps." Minna and the dog were left behind in Zurich when Wagner went to London, and, on his return, he found his four-footed friend ailing. The faithful animal pulled himself together, gave him a friendly greeting, and for a short while under the excitement of his master's return seemed to revive somewhat, but relapsed. The Wagners had been invited to dine at the Wesendonks' on the 9th of July, but Wagner could not be persuaded to leave his sick animal friend.

"I fear my dear faithful friend—my Peps —is going to die to-day. It is impossible for me to desert the poor creature in his dying moments. Do not, therefore, be annoyed if we beg of you to dine without us to-day. . . . Surely you will not laugh at me when I tell you that I am weeping."

Peps actually died that night. Wagner was with him almost continuously, and he buried the dog with his own hands in the garden in the rear of the house.

Wagner's footing in the Wesendonk family was becoming more intimate, a fact to which he refers humorously in a letter in which

32

he transmits a copy of Grimm's "Fairy Tales" to Mathilde.

"You see, you cannot rid yourself of me so easily. I am so securely nested in your house that even if you were to burn it down a familiar voice would call out to you from among the salvage, 'It was about time we got out of this!'"

THE VILLA ON THE GREEN HILL

The Wesendonks entered into their beautiful villa on the Green Hill overlooking the lake of Zurich, on August 22, 1857. The mutual friend of Wagner and Mathilde, Frau Eliza Wille, a novelist, and the wife of the philosopher and Orientalist, François Wille, who lived in Mariafeld not far from Zurich, has left a description of the hospitality which prevailed at the villa. "It was a period of almost clarified existence for all who met in the beautiful villa on the Green Hill. Wealth, taste and elegance served to beautify life there. The host was unhampered in seeking to advance everything in which he took an interest, and full of admiration for the extraordinary man whom Fate had led into his circle.

33

" The hostess, young and tender-hearted, and an idealist, knew no more of the world and of life than if these had been the surface of a gently flowing river. Beloved and admired by her husband, a young, happy mother, she lived in the admiration of whatever was important in art and life, and of all that power of genius which never before had she beheld as now in the very act of inspiration and creation. The arrangements of the house, the wealth of its owner, made possible there a social intercourse, to which every one of those who were fortunate enough to enjoy it ever will look back with delight."

MATHILDE "A LOVELY BEING"

Wagner's friend, Richard Pohl, says that the composer was in daily intercourse with the Wesendonks. He speaks of Mathilde as a lovely being, a graceful, womanly and poetically inclined nature, who exercised a manifestly stimulating influence over the master. He adds that compared with her, Wagner's wife Minna, who had aged rapidly, naturally was thrown into the shade; that in Wagner's presence Minna usually was quiet, but freely vented her opinions when he was not about.

The Wesendonk Villa in Zurich

She could not understand why her husband
occupied himself for years with projects for
which there was not the slightest prospect
of realisation. Upon the "Nibelung" project she based no hopes at all. She would
much have preferred compositions which
would have found easy acceptance everywhere and have brought in money. "That
there could be no harmony between two such
natures was manifest at a glance," says Pohl;
and he adds: "That sooner or later a separation would have to take place could be
prophesied without difficulty."

NEARING THE DANGER LINE

From these characterisations it is easy to
discover why Mathilde exercised such an influence upon the composer, and why he was
obliged to seek artistic sympathy outside of
his own home. But there is always a danger
line in such a proceeding, and both he who
was seeking sympathy and she who was
lavishing it upon him rapidly were nearing
that line.

Wagner moved into the châlet, which he
feelingly called his "Asyl" (Retreat) late

in April, 1857. "Ten days ago," he writes
to Liszt under date of May 8, "we took
possession of the little country house next to
the Wesendonks' villa, which I owe to the
great sympathy of that friendly family. At
first I had to go through various troubles;
for the furnishing of the little house, which
has turned out very well indeed and according to my taste, took much time, and we had
to move out from our former quarters before
there was any possibility of moving in. . .
For ten days we lived at the hotel; and at last
we moved in here in very cold and horrid
weather. Only the thought that the change
would be definite was able to keep me in good
temper. At last we have got through it all;
everything is permanently housed and arranged according to wish and need; everything is in the place where it is to remain. My
study has been ordered with the pedantic for-
mality and elegant comfort with which you
are familiar. My writing table stands at
the large window, with a splendid view of the
lake and the Alps; rest and quiet surround
me. A pretty and well-stocked garden offers
little walks and resting places to me, and will
enable my wife to occupy herself pleasantly,

and to keep herself free from troubling thoughts about me."

"TROUBLING THOUGHTS"

Attention may be called to two points in this letter. He speaks of being indebted for the châlet to the great sympathy of the Wesendonks. In point of fact, it was Mathilde who really secured it for him, and I mention this as an example of the tact which Wagner always shows whenever he refers to women in his letters. In the course of his life he made numerous conquests of the heart, yet in all his correspondence I do not know of a single sentence in which he boasts of any of these.

"Will enable my wife to occupy herself pleasantly and to keep herself free from troubling thoughts about me." Minna was delighted with the châlet and its surroundings, and could have been happy there for the rest of her life, but—she already was furiously jealous of Mathilde. These were the "troubling thoughts," and they played their part in the catastrophe which followed. Wagner believed he had found a permanent "Retreat" in this lovely demesne, but the tragedy

which again made him a homeless wanderer
for many years was only a little more than a
year in coming.

" TRISTAN " TO THE FORE

It has been seen that in July, 1857, having
completed the second act of " Siegfried," and
sketched out the third, Wagner definitely laid
aside " The Ring of the Nibelung," not to
take it up again until 1869. The reason?
Inspired by Mathilde, he threw himself heart
and soul into " Tristan und Isolde."

He had had the subject in mind before. In
1854 he touched on it in a letter to Liszt. " As
I never in life have felt the real bliss of love "
(this after eighteen years of matrimony!)
" I must erect a monument to the most beautiful of all my dreams, in which from the beginning to end that love shall be thoroughly
satiated. I have in my head ' Tristan und
Isolde,' the simplest and most full-blooded
musical conception, and with the ' black flag '
which floats at the end of it I shall cover
myself to die." At the same time, however,
he states that he must finish his " Nibelung "
scores. " ' Die Walküre ' has taken so much
out of me that I must indulge in this pleas-

ure." At that time evidently " Tristan " was not to interfere with the " Ring " and was not to be taken up seriously until the last stroke of the pen on " Götterdämmerung."

THE ACCENT OF PASSION

Mathilde's influence in 1854 was not as potent as it had become in 1857. She did not yet fill the vision of his soul so completely, and the renunciation which was to be his lot did not as yet cry out for the consummation of that which he was obliged to renounce. " Tristan und Isolde," as originally conceived by Wagner, as he wrote to Liszt, was to be a drama of satiety. Mathilde made it what it is—a drama, *the* drama, of passionate renunciation. For it is what we desire but cannot possess that demands the accent of passion, whereas possession gives repose. Desire is the red rose, possession the white.

Even before he definitely laid aside the " Nibelung " compositions for " Tristan " Wagner also had the " Parsifal " legend in mind, as well as the material for a Buddhistic subject to be called " Die Sieger " (The Victors). Parsifal, however, was not to be the hero of a separate drama, but to figure in

39

"Tristan und Isolde," passing through
Kareol in his quest for the Grail, and paus-
ing at the couch of the wounded Tristan.
Later Wagner eliminated this episode and decided to make Parsifal the subject of a drama
by itself. At that time, and for many years
later, he refers to the Grail seeker as Parzival, and this spelling obtains until 1877,
when he finally settled upon Parsifal (literally meaning the "guileless fool").

"TRISTAN" IN FULL SWING

We have seen that Wagner moved into his
châlet late in April. A letter to Liszt, written during the following month, shows
"Siegfried" abandoned and "Tristan"
already in full swing. The enthusiasm with
which he worked on this new conception proves
how much it engrossed his mind and heart.
He sketched out the entire story in prose, and
this first synopsis of the drama was duly presented to his Isolde. One can hardly believe
it, but, although this prose-sketch is dated
August 20, 1857, the drama in its poetic
form was ready to be presented to Mathilde
on the 18th of September! That it should
have been written apparently in less than a

month seems marvellous, the more so, as the changes between this first manuscript and the final form of the poem are very slight. Then he began the composition of the music, and, as it bloomed in his soul, flower after flower of his muse was sent to her who inspired their fragrance.

"DREAMS"

How did Mathilde respond? Was the sovereign need of love beginning to assert itself in her? It would seem so. For in return for the poem of "Tristan und Isolde" and the music which pulsated with her own heart beats, she sent Wagner five poems which she had written and in which she seems to break silence with herself and to give expression to feelings long hidden in the depths of a soul that yearned to respond to her Tristan's love rhapsody. She, too, was moved to dare; yet a secret presentiment appears to have warned her of the consequences. It would seem to permeate at least one of the poems:

IN THE GREEN HOUSE

High vaulted verdure, crowns of foliage,
Canopies of emerald, offspring of distant zones,
Tell me, why do you murmur?

41

Silently your branches droop, you trace in the air
    unchangeable images.
Symbols of suffering, gentle perfumes
Rising from your chalices.
In the languor of your desire your branches open
    like arms,
But you are captives of illusion, your embraces only
    shadows and fears.

Ah, poor verdure, I too, know; we share the same
    fate.
Not in this brilliant sunlight—our country is not
    here!
The sun shines without regret in the splendor of a
    desolate day.
He who suffers deeply is enveloped in shadow and
    silence.
All is still, and chilling air touches the glass house.
On the edge of the tender leaves I see trembling
    heavy drops.

Among these five poems was the famous
" Dreams." Wagner seized upon it with
avidity. Indeed, he threw himself heart and
soul into the musical setting of these lines.
It was this song which was destined to become
the foundation of the great love-duet in the
second act of " Tristan." Through it, and
thus through Mathilde, he discovered the
musical soul of " Tristan und Isolde," for
" Tristan und Isolde " is one great heart throb

up to the love duet, and, after it, one great
heart throb down to death.

A TRIUMPH OF ART THROUGH LOVE

" Dreams " was a triumph of art achieved
through love. How could it fail to make him
feel more ardently than ever what Mathilde
was to him? Not satisfied with setting the
poem to song, but desiring to render deeper
homage to the woman who had inspired his
music, he arranged it for orchestra, and on
the 23d of December, 1857, Mathilde's birthday, had it played for her in her house as a
morning greeting for the new year on which
her life was entering. Another such musical
tribute has not been laid at the feet of woman.
Even the " Siegfried Idyll," which years later
Wagner composed for Cosima, is not to be
compared with this burst of impassioned
song—the musical soul of a great tragedy.
" Dreams " and " In the Green House," Wagner himself called studies to " Tristan und
Isolde."

The atmosphere between the châlet and the
villa was becoming more and more charged
with emotional electricity. Unspoken messages were flying thither and back long before

the days of " wireless." The beautiful woman
of the Green Hill was sensitised to every
thought and feeling of the genius in the
châlet. The relation was idealised. She was
uplifting and comforting a sorrowing soul.
But " Dreams? "—She was caught in its
flood of music and almost swept away.

For from the moment " Siegfried " was laid
aside and " Tristan " taken up in earnest, one
can read the reason in the lines and between
the lines of every communication that passed
from châlet to villa.

Mathilde sent Wagner a silken pillow for
his couch.

" Ah! The blissful pillow! " he exclaims.
" So soft, so delicate! Tired and heavy as
my head oft is, I have not dared to rest it
there, not even when I have been ill;—only in
death. Then I may bed it in luxury, as if it
were my right! Then you shall smooth the
pillow under my head. There you have my
last will and testament."

HIS MUSE—AND HIS ISOLDE

She was at once his Isolde and his muse:
" And my lovely muse still remains distant.
Silently I await her visit; I do not wish to

disquiet her by petitioning her. For the muse, like love, is a voluntary benefactress. Unhappy fool he who would try to win her forcibly when she does not give herself up to him of her own free will. You will not allow yourself to be forcibly drawn to me. Is it not so? Is it not so? How could love be muse if it yielded to force? And my dear, sweet muse still absents herself."

A DEDICATION

Then followed at various times brief announcements of the progress of "Tristan." "The great duet, Tristan and Isolde's outburst," he writes her, "has turned out beautiful beyond all measure. At this moment in great joy over it."

On the 31st of December, 1857, she received the entire musical sketch of the first act with these lines:

"Through bliss elated,
Sorrow abated,
Pure and free
E'er to thee;
How sorely tried,
Whate'er denied,
Tristan and Isolden
In tones so chaste and golden,

45

Their tears and kisses sweet,
I lay them at thy feet,
That they, the angel seeing,
Praise thee who gave me being."

These verses are somewhat freely translated, but that Wagner regarded Mathilde as one through whom his soul had been born anew is shown by a passage in one of his letters recalling a certain moment that passed between them as " Life," whereas all that had gone before was but the prelude and all that had followed but the postlude of his life—a passage, however, which I will not anticipate by quoting now.

" HIS EYES ON MINE WERE FASTENED!"

Well might Wagner call Mathilde his " Muse," well might he write her the lines which she received with the first act of " Tristan." Not only did she write " Dreams," she also suggested to him one of the most poetic changes which he made in the old " Tristan " legend when he remoulded it in the crucible of his genius. In the legend it is the drinking of the potion which excites the love of Tristan and Isolde. Mathilde, sensitive, refined, psychic, saw in this a basis that

46

was too artificial. At her suggestion Tristan and Isolde loved from the moment their glances met for the first time. Wonderful insight of woman!

PREMONITIONS?

Wagner and Mathilde were two beings hedged round by the conventions of the nineteenth century, yet daring to lay bare their souls to each other. Their glances, too, had met. Had neither of them a presentiment of danger? Read "In the Green House," and note the woman's premonition. There is some evidence that Wagner too was aware of the peril in which they stood; also that, feeling himself bound to Mathilde's husband by ties of gratitude and friendship, he endeavoured to escape it. He made a hurried trip to Paris, pleading business reasons which always have seemed insufficient to justify his going. Moreover he could ill afford the expense. But through what we now know of Wagner and his Isolde, the trip appears in a different and more plausible light. It was an attempt to remove himself from the danger zone. But this effort to interne his heart on neutral territory was futile. The longing for love was irresistible. Liszt was telegraphed to for money and Wagner hurried back to Zurich and Isolde faster than he had left them.

THE IVORY BATON

Events now follow each other rapidly. The air is charged with impending catastrophe.

There had not yet been at the villa a formal house-warming, or as the Germans call it more feelingly, Hausweihe (consecration of the house). For this ceremony Wagner, at the request of the Wesendonks, arranged a concert, which took place on the 31st of March, 1858, in the foyer of the villa art gallery. The programme consisted of Beethoven selections, Wagner conducted, and there was an audience of about one hundred people. One can readily imagine the numerous meetings for the discussing of plans and the thousand and one details connected with the concert which constantly brought Wagner and Mathilde together.

At the concert there was a presentation ceremony, Mathilde presenting Wagner with an ivory baton, which she told him she had had made expressly for him in Paris. No tragedy is wholly without its humorous side-play, and this incident forms the one amusing touch in the story of Wagner and his Isolde. Mathilde was guilty of a little pious fraud in the affair of the ivory baton. She well knew her inspired friend's expensive tastes. Hence the Paris version of the baton. Mathilde had indeed ordered it especially made for Wagner—but in Zurich.

BUSY TONGUES

The concert, the presentation, Wagner's removal to the châlet, his constant visits at the villa, his manifest intimacy there, the frequency with which he was seen with Mathilde, started all the gossips of Zurich going. In the cafés Orsino and Rüden the nobility and the professors of the University gloated over the affair; in the Litteraire the German contingent moralised over it in a heavy way; in the Zunfthäuser the men of Zurich looked wise when it was mentioned; in their sitting-rooms, their kitchens, and at chance meetings on the lower bridge the women of the town, none too blessed with good looks themselves, and to whom " pretty 'Thilde of the Green Hill " was an object of envy, tore her reputation to tatters.

49

THE AWAKENING

Meanwhile what was transpiring in the " Retreat," and in the villa? About this time Von Bülow wrote to a friend, " From Zurich comes hopeless news. Wagner is in terrible financial straits. I imagine that something has gone wrong between him and the Wesendonks."

This suggests that the query, " What was transpiring in the ' Retreat,' and in the villa? " should be changed to " What *had* transpired in the ' Retreat,' and in the villa?"

In July, 1858, the exact date not having been preserved, Wagner sent Mathilde these lines—brief, but how significant: " What a wonderful birth for our child of pain! [This refers to " Tristan und Isolde."] After all, it seems we must keep on living. Of whom could it be demanded that he desert his children? God be with us wretched ones! Or are we too blessed? Are we the only ones who can help ourselves? "

Again, what had transpired on the Green Hill? No biographer has been able to answer that question until now. But if we look ahead in the journal which Wagner kept after he had fled from Zurich to Venice, a journal destined for Mathilde's eyes, and hers only, these hints are discoverable:

" A year ago to-day," he writes September 18, 1858, " I finished my ' Tristan ' poem and took the last act to you. You led me to the chair near the sofa, embraced me and said ' Now I have nothing more to wish for.' "

And again on October 1, 1858, he wrote: " You, my child, I no longer pity . . . No longer do you look upon your grief as wholly your own, but as a part of the sorrow of the world . . . But, ah! how I pitied you at that moment when you had thrust me from you, when no longer the victim of sorrow, but of passionate desire, you thought yourself betrayed and your noblest feelings misinterpreted. At that moment you appeared to me like an angel whose God had deserted her."

ON THE BRINK

Mathilde and her poet-composer had faced each other on the brink. Wagner says, in so many words, that she thrust him from her, that at the crisis of her life her purity saved her—that she was like one " betrayed," like

" an angel whose God had deserted her."
However vibrant her soul, however keen in re-
sponse to Wagner's every thought and feeling, she was a wife and mother. Wagner
may have been her passion—but, at the critical moment, her love harked back to Otto and
the children. Possibly, too, her aristocratic
instinct came to her rescue. Women of her
wealth and position are of two kinds. The
one sacrifices everything and goes forth into
the night. The other considers and waits for
daylight. May not Mathilde, in imagination, have heard the' door of the villa
close forever behind her, and in the click of
the lock discerned the note of warning that
her beautiful romance could end only in
poverty and a sordid struggle for existence?
I, for one (and I believe the world is with
me), am glad that we can remember her as
the proud mistress of the Green Hill, instead
of as the successor of Minna in the kitchen.

CATASTROPHE

What Wagner has hinted at was a catas-
trophe, but not *the* catastrophe. In that
Minna had a hand. Furiously jealous of
Mathilde, she broke through all restraints

and created a " scene " in the villa itself. It
resulted not only in Wagner's leaving Zurich,
but also in his separation from Minna. He
went his lonely way to Venice; she sought
refuge with his sister Clara in Dresden. Fortunately it is possible to give Wagner's version of the affair in his own words.

The separation was so sudden that he had no
time to more than merely apprise Clara that
she might expect his wife, consequently his
sister wrote to him, requesting a " brotherly
explanation." He replied in a long letter
dated August 20, 1858, and probably written
from Geneva, where he had stopped en route
for Venice. It is profoundly interesting because in it he analyses his relations with Mathilde, and from his own view-point, of course,
Minna's attitude toward the affair.

WAGNER'S OWN VERSION

" What has preserved, consoled, and even
strengthened me during these last six years,
. . . has been the love of this young
woman, which, at first timorous, doubting,
hesitating, and bashful, at last went out
toward me with ever increasing directness and
certainty. As there could be no question of

a union between us, our deep affection partook of the character of that sad, sweet longing which keeps everything vulgar and low at a distance, and found its chief source of compensation in our mutual welfare. From the very beginning of our acquaintance she has shown the most tireless and delicately expressed interest in me, and has courageously interceded with her husband for everything that could make life easier for me. This love, which had remained unspoken between us, finally had to show itself openly, when last year I wrote ' Tristan,' and presented her with the poem. Then for the first time she became powerless, and declared to me that nothing remained for her but to die!

" Imagine, dear sister, what this love meant to me, after a life like mine of trouble and sorrow, excitement and self-denial. But at the same time we realised that such a thing as a closer union between us was impossible, and, smothering our selfish desire in a spirit of resignation, we suffered, bore our burdens, but—loved!

" With clever womanly instinct, my wife seemed to understand how matters stood. At times she was jealous, mocking, contemptuous, but she tolerated our intercourse, which, after all, did not violate the conventions and only looked toward the possibility of feeling that we were in each other's presence. Therefore I concluded that Minna was sensible and that she understood she had nothing to fear because there could be no thought of closer relations; moreover, that she deemed it advisable, in fact, the best thing she could do, to shut her eyes to what was going on. But I was to find out how mistaken I had been. Gossip was rife, and at last my wife so far forgot herself that she intercepted one of my letters and opened it. If she had been able to fully understand this letter it would really have given her the desired sense of security, for our feeling of resignation was its theme. But she had eyes only for the intimate expressions, and lost her senses. She met me in a rage, and thus forced me to explain to her with calmness, but determination, how matters stood; that she had brought this misfortune upon herself, in having dared to open such a letter; and that if she did not contain herself, it would be necessary for us to separate. On this we agreed, I calmly, she angrily. But the next day I felt sorry for her. I sought her

out and said, ' Minna, you are very ill! Get
well and then let us talk this matter over
again.'

MINNA MAKES A SCENE

"We agreed that she should take the cure
somewhere. She seemed to quiet down, and
the time for her departure arrived. She insisted, however, that she must have a meeting
with Mme. Wesendonk before leaving. This
I most decidedly forbade her. It was of the
highest importance for me to try to explain
to Minna gradually the exact nature of the
relations to which she objected, and to make
it clear to her that she had nothing to fear
so far as the continuance of our married life
was concerned, if only she would behave herself reasonably, and, in a high-minded way,
give up any idea of revenge, and avoid anything like a scene.

"Finally she promised this, but she did not
rest. Behind my back she went to Mme. Wesendonk and—probably without appreciating
the consequences—insulted the refined woman
in a most abominable manner. When she said,
' If I were an ordinary woman I would show
this letter to your husband!' there was no

other recourse for Mme. Wesendonk, who was
conscious of never having kept a secret from
her husband (which, of course, a woman like
Minna cannot understand!) but to tell him
at once of this scene and what had led to it.
The delicacy and purity of our relations having thus been attacked in a rude and vulgar
way, a great change became necessary. It
required a long time for me to persuade my
friend that a nature like my wife's could not
be made to comprehend such high-minded and
unselfish relations as existed between us, for I
was met with her earnest, deep-felt reproof,
that whereas she always had taken her husband into her confidence, I had not done so
with my wife.

" Whoever can appreciate what I have suffered since then (all this occurred in the middle of April), also can imagine what my feelings must be now I realise that my strenuous
efforts to resume the disturbed relations have
been fruitless. For three months, while Minna
was taking the cure, I showed every consideration for her peace of mind. In order that she
might quiet down, I refrained, during this
period, from all intercourse with our neigh-
bours. Concerned only for her welfare, I did

everything to bring her to her senses and to a point of view that would become her and her age. All in vain! She persists in the most trivial misrepresentations, declares herself insulted, and, while calmer at times, again breaks out into rage as before. Last month, Minna having returned because we had visitors, it was necessary to reach some decision. It was impossible that these two women could continue living so near together, for Mme. Wesendonk, on her side, could not forget that the great sacrifices she had made for me and the delicate regard she had shown me had been repaid by me, through my wife, with a gross insult."

WESENDONK JEALOUS

The guests to whom Wagner refers in this letter were, oddly enough, the Von Bülows, Hans and Cosima, the latter Liszt's daughter, who, some years later, left her husband, cast her lot with Wagner, and eventually became the power behind the throne at Bayreuth. They were witnesses of some of the violent scenes which disrupted the Wagner household, but there is nothing in Von Bülow's letters to indicate that he appreciated the real

OTTO WESENDONK
1860
From a photograph taken in Rome

cause of the composer's leaving Zurich and of his separation from Minna.

Interesting as is the letter from Wagner to his sister as it stands in the German edition of the Wagner-Wesendonk book, the editor has, with too evident purpose, omitted several significant passages, in which Wagner refers to increasing jealousy on the part of Wesendonk, " with whom it finally became a question of preserving the mother of his children," who, Wagner adds, were " unconscious obstacles " between Mathilde and himself. The outcome seems to prove that Otto managed the affair with infinite tact. Instead of spoiling matters by ill-timed displays of temper, he awaited the right moment and then sent Wagner flying, apparently with Mathilde's consent. The woman who appears to her lover " like an angel whose God has deserted her," is apt to be grateful when she discovers that her husband hasn't.

FLIGHT

Wagner's departure from Zurich was precipitate. In fact it resembled headlong flight rather than premeditated departure. He had no time to communicate with many of his most intimate friends there and in the neighbourhood, like the Willes, Keller, and Herwegh, the poet. He was expecting a visit from Liszt on August 20, but although only three days remained until that date, he fled—August 17, 1858.

"When you can spare a quiet hour," Liszt wrote to him on the 26th of the same month, "let me know why you did not care to stay a few days longer at Zurich where I intended to visit you on the 20th inst. at the latest." There is no evidence in the Wagner-Liszt correspondence that the explanation was forthcoming—another indication of Wagner's delicate reticence regarding his affairs with women.

Why did Wagner's efforts at smoothing things over between the châlet and the Green Hill fail? He even had called in the Princess Sayn-Wittgenstein, Liszt's *amie*, and asked her for advice. She, thinking Mathilde was in the same boat as herself, wrote a decidedly Delphic opinion on what she supposed to be the situation. There is reason to believe that Wagner's swift departure from the "Retreat," in which he had expected to pass the remainder of his life in peace and comfort, was due to the fact that the gossip of Zurich became too much for Otto. The husband always is the last person to hear the scandal that affects his honour, but when he does, it is not meted out to him on the instalment plan. Finck, in his "Wagner and his Works," which justly has been called a masterpiece, says that Wesendonk ordered the composer out of the châlet and out of Zurich. Bélart, who, before he constructed his brochure, "Richard Wagner in Zurich," went over the ground with a fine-tooth comb, gathering up every detail that came in his way, writes:

"A brief and vehement passage of words between Wagner and Wesendonk, a few sharp commands from the latter—so says tradition—and Wagner's fate was sealed."

The composer's friend, Jacob Sulzer, an ex-official of the town, and the Kurwenal of the Zurich tragedy (Mathilde refers to him as the "Getreuesten aller Getreuen"—the most faithful of the faithful), loaned him money to reach Geneva, where he borrowed the sum that carried him to Venice, his efforts to raise the necessary amount even leading him to apply for a loan to a barber who had shaved him in Zurich.

We know that Minna was furiously jealous of Mathilde; but it is possible, also, to quote in her own words her opinion of that lady. The following winter, when the Wesendonks lost their son Guido, Minna wrote this comment to a friend: " The news of the death of little Guido, youngest son of the Wesendonks, has depressed me terribly. I believe it is but the dispensation of Providence that God visits affliction on this heartless woman spoiled by a happy life. How many times have I hoped that the Lord would bring about a change in her through the sickness of one of her children; but see! I still tremble with the terror of the thought." Minna once referred to Tristan and Isolde as " a nasty, love-sick pair."

LAST MESSAGE FROM THE " RETREAT "

Wagner's last messages to Mathilde from the " Retreat " were inexpressibly sad. A short time before the final break, but when he must have realised that it was impending, he wrote her a long letter, from which I quote the most significant phrases:

" Surely you do not expect that I will allow
your wonderfully beautiful and glorious
letter to remain unanswered? Or should I
have denied myself the privilege of replying
to your noble utterance? Yet how can I
reply in manner worthy of you?

" The terrible struggles through which I
have passed, how could they end otherwise
than in complete victory over all longing and
desire?

" Were we not forwarned in the warmest
moments of mutual attraction that such would
be our ultimate goal?

" Surely, because it was so difficult, so un-
heard of—that was the very reason why it
could be attained only after the severest struggles. Have we not now reached the end of
these? Or are there others still awaiting
us? Surely, I feel it deeply, they are at an
end!

" Only a month ago I told your husband of
my decision to break off all personal intercourse with you. I had renounced you, but
I had not come to a complete understanding
with my own self. I felt that only through
a complete separation, or a complete union,
could we protect our love against the dreaded

contact that threatened it so recently. On one side was the necessity for a separation, on the other the possibility of a closer relation which, even if not desired, still lured our thoughts. Herein lay the painful stress which was too great for us to bear. I came into your presence, and at once we realised clearly and forever that that other possibility would be an outrage which we ourselves should not tolerate.

"Turn again to the world I cannot; that I should settle for any definite length of time in a large city is unthinkable; and should I, on the other hand, seek for myself a new 'Retreat,' another hearth, when I am obliged to leave in ruins behind me the one which friendship and exalted love had provided for me in this exquisite paradise? No!—For me to go from here is to go under!

"With these wounds in my heart, I cannot even attempt to found another home!

"My child, I can think of but one salvation for myself, and this cannot be secured to me through material surroundings, but must come from the innermost depths of my heart. It is repose of soul! Suppression of all longing! Quenching of all desire! Noble, worthy conquest of self! Living for others—for others to our own consolation!

"PRAY FOR ME IN SILENCE"

" Now you will comprehend the grave, decisive conclusion which, inwardly, I have reached. It colours my whole view of life, my whole future, everything I value—and so, too, my attitude toward you, who are dearest of all to me! Let it be granted to me that thus from among the ruins of this world of desire—I still may prove a blessing to you! Behold, never in my life, under no circumstances, have I been forward, but on the contrary, almost too reserved. Now, for the first time I shall appear too insistent of your welfare in begging you to be inwardly reassured concerning me. I shall not visit you very often, for from now on you are to see me only when I am sure that I can meet you with a cheerful, calm countenance.—Formerly I sought you out in sorrow and longing. Whither I went for consolation, thither I brought unrest and pain. Thus if you do not see me during longer periods of time—pray for me in silence—for know then that I am suffering! But if I do come, then be assured

65

that I shall bear to you a gracious gift from my inner self, a gift to bestow which is reserved for me alone, who have taken upon myself to suffer so much.

" My child, the latter months have perceptibly whitened the hair about my temples. A voice within me calls me longingly to rest— the rest which years ago I caused my Flying Dutchman to long for. It was a longing for —'Home'—not for the ecstacy of sensuous love! A woman, faithful, blessed, alone could win that home for him. Let us offer a sacrifice to that beautiful death which is the refuge and amelioration of all our longing and desire! Let us, calm and glorified, face that blessed death with the blissful smile of exquisite self-denial! And—no one will be the loser if we—conquer! Farewell, my beloved, blessed angel! "

" FAREWELL! "

A little later she received this one line written in English, " It must be so ! " and, doubtless on his last evening in the " Retreat," though the exact date is missing, came his last message to her from the châlet:

" Farewell, farewell, beloved! I part in peace.
Wherever I am, there I shall be wholly yours,
Seek to preserve the ' Retreat' for me.
Aufwiedersehen! Aufwiedersehen! dear soul of my
    soul! Farewell! Aufwiedersehen!
Farewell! Aufwiedersehen!"

The following morning the door of the " Retreat " closed behind him. He never set foot in it again.

A LONELY EXILE IN VENICE

II

AFTER Wagner left Zurich no direct communication passed between him and the Wesendonk family until the following January. Soon after reaching Venice he wrote to Mathilde, but the latter sent the letter unopened to Frau Wille, who returned it to Wagner. Yet relations were not wholly severed. Beginning shortly after his flight from the " Retreat," and after he reached Geneva, Wagner started a journal or diary, in which he put down his most intimate thoughts, and which was intended for Mathilde. This journal and a second one were, in fact, eventually sent to Frau Wille, and by her transmitted to the Green Hill. They have been preserved with this correspondence. Mathilde, on her side, also kept a journal, which Frau Wille sent to Wagner, but which has not been preserved. Wagner's journal not only fixes the date of his departure from Zurich, but also settles the point as to whether that departure was voluntary or precipitate. Much dust has been thrown in the public's eyes in regard to this. Thus Glasenapp, Wagner's official biographer, calmly states that the composer left Zurich in order to settle in some place where there would be greater opportunity of hearing his own music. Imagine choosing Venice for that! Wagner wrote these lines over his diary:

" JOURNAL
SINCE MY FLIGHT FROM THE RETREAT
17th August, 1858."

He himself thus characterised his departure from Zurich as " Flucht " (flight).

Wagner begins his journal with a gloomy analysis of his suffering during the last night in the " Retreat," and follows it with a realistic description of his parting from Minna. Altogether there are three entries in the journal dated from Geneva.

"THUS LOOKING UP TO YOU I DIED"
Geneva, August 21, 1858.

The last night in the " Retreat " I went to bed at eleven o'clock ; I was to leave the next morning at five. Before I closed my eyes I

recalled how I had been accustomed to woo
sleep on this spot by making the mental
presentation that there I was destined to
breathe my last. Thus I would lie there when
you should enter to me for the last time, when
you, fearlessly before all, should hold me
close in your embrace and with my last kiss
receive my soul! This death was the most
beautiful of my imaginings, and I had pic-
tured it entirely with reference to the arrangement of my bedchamber. The door
toward the stairs was closed, you entered
through the portière of my study. And thus
you twined your arms about me, and thus,
looking up to you, I died.

And now? Even the possibility of thus passing away is taken from me. Chilled, and like
one hunted, I left this abode, where I had been
locked in with my evil spirit whom I no longer
could save by flight. Where—where can I
die now?—and so I fell asleep.

"INTO UTTER LONELINESS"

. . . And now I had taken leave. Now
everything was cold and irresponsive in me—
I went downstairs. There my wife awaited
me. She offered me tea. It was a frightfully

wretched moment. She accompanied me. We
descended into the garden. It was a glorious
morning. I did not look about me. At the
final parting there was a burst of grief and
tears from my wife. For the first time my
eyes remained dry. I counselled her again
to bear herself gently and nobly, and to seek
Christian consolation. The same vengeful
violence again flared up in her. She is beyond saving, I was obliged to acknowledge to
myself. But—I cannot wreak vengeance
upon the unfortunate woman. Let her pro-
nounce judgment upon herself.—I was fearfully in earnest and bitter, and sad, but—
weep I could not.—Thus she journeyed away.
And behold!—I will not deny that I felt re-
lieved, that I breathed freely again.—I have
passed into utter loneliness.—There I am at
home; there where with every breath I may
love you!

Yesterday I wrote to my sister Clara, whom
you met two years ago. She requested a
brotherly explanation of me; for I had written her and announced Minna's coming. I
gave her an inkling of what you had been to
me during these last six years, and still were;
the heavenly refuge you had vouchsafed me,

at the expense of what sacrifices and struggles you have protected me; and what a
rough, rude hand had now been laid on this
wonder work of your noble and exalted love. I
am sure she understands me. She is an enthusiastic soul in a somewhat neglected frame.
I was obliged to make some explanation in
that direction, but how heart and soul
trembled as I wrote her these things, and was
enabled at the same time to touch delicately
upon your high-mindedness, nobility and
purity!—Surely we shall forget all this, and
find consolation for our grief, and only the
supreme consciousness will remain that here
was a miracle such as nature permits only
once in the course of centuries, and never perhaps with such exquisite success. Away with
sorrow! After all, we are supremely happy!
With whom would we exchange?

A DREAM PICTURE

August 23, 1858, 5 a. m.

In my dreams I saw you on the terrace.
You were in male attire, with a travelling cap
on your head, and peering in the direction I
had taken, but I was approaching from

another point. Thus your eyes always were
turned away from me, while I was striving
to let you know that I was near. Softly I
called "Mathilde!" Then louder and
louder, till my bedroom re-echoed with the
cry, and my own shouts awoke me.—When
later on I again managed to get a little sleep,
and began to dream, I read letters from you,
in which you confessed a youthful love affair
to me.

You had renounced your lover, yet you
were praising his good qualities to me. I
felt as if I had been called in simply to console you—which rather piqued me. To avoid
the recurrence of this dream, I got up and
wrote these lines—during which a violent
longing and grievous impatience again have
taken possession of me.

August 24, 1858.

Yesterday I was in the depths of woe. Why
continue to live? Why live? Is it cowardice
—or courage?—Why does life raise us to
the heights of bliss only to steep us in the
depths of woe? I slept soundly this past
night—to-day things are better.—I have
had made for myself here a fine portfolio

with a lock and key, and solely for souvenirs of you, and for your letters. It will hold a great deal, and whatever goes into it never shall be returned to the naughty child, so be careful what you send me. You will get nothing back—except after my death, and then only in case you will not permit it to be buried with me.

WRITES TO FRAU WILLE

Venice was the objective of Wagner's flight. There he hoped to find some consolation in new impressions, and also quiet and leisure to proceed with " Tristan."

First, however, he was obliged to ascertain whether it would be a safe refuge for him. At that time Venice was an Austrian possession and there was danger that the Saxon authorities, under whose ban he still was, might seek and obtain his extradition. As the result of inquiries instituted by Liszt, and independently by himself, he felt assured of his safety. The necessity of making these inquiries and of borrowing money detained him in Geneva until August 25th. The first Venetian entry in his journal is under September 3, 1858, and in it he mentions having written to Mathilde on the previous day.

Before quoting from the journal, however, it seems best, for several reasons, to give the letter which he wrote to Frau Wille on September 30. The letter he had despatched to his Isolde had been returned to him unopened by Frau Wille. Evidently Wesendonk deemed it best that, for the present at least, all direct communication between his wife and Wagner should cease. Therefore, the only way that remained for him to let her know how he was situated in Venice was for him to write to their mutual friend in Mariafeld and trust to the latter to get the letter into Mathilde's hands. It must have reached her, otherwise it would not have been included in the correspondence.

This letter is extremely interesting because in it Wagner gives, in addition to bitter comments on the world in general and his own fate, a description of his quarters in the Palazzo Giustiniani, and also locates that structure. This is of some importance, because there were at that time four Giustiniani palaces in Venice, and at least one of the leading guidebooks has associated the wrong one—

that which subsequently became the European Hotel—with Wagner's sojourn in 1858-59. The composer's description shows clearly that he resided considerably farther along the Grand Canal, and on the opposite side of that waterway, in the Palazzo Giustiniani which adjoins the Palazzo Foscari. The letter also gives in a few wonderfully poetic touches his impressions of the city of the lagoons, the concluding passages being simply exquisite.

"EVERYTHING STRANGE AND COLD!"

" The world merely looks on the practical side of things," writes Wagner. " With me, however, the ideal is so much the real that it forms a reality I cannot bear to have disturbed. Now at last, at the age of forty-six, I am forced to acknowledge that my sole comfort is to be found in solitude and that I must stand apart by myself.

" Everything around me strange and cold! No soothing influence, no glance, no comforting voice. I have sworn that I will not even keep a dog. Nothing that may become dear to me shall be about me. She at least has her children!

" That is no reproach! Only a plaint; and
I think she will gladly take me as I am, and
harken to my lament.

" She helps me so sweetly! What a heavenly
letter from her you sent me to-day! Dear,
lovely soul—may she be comforted! Her
friend is faithful to her, lives only through
her—and, for that reason only, is able to
bear up!

" My palace lies about halfway between the
Piazzetta and the Rialto, near the sharp bend
which the canal makes around the Palazzo
Foscari (now an armoury), next door to me.
Diagonally opposite me is the Palazzo Grassi.
. . . My landlord is an Austrian who, on
account of my famous name, received me enthusiastically, and is extraordinarily clever
and obliging in everything. (He it was who
caused my arrival here to be announced in all
the newspapers.) You probably have read
that my coming here is regarded as a political
chess move on my part, with the ultimate
object of cautiously working my way back
to Germany through Austria. Even friend
Liszt was of this opinion, and, at the same
time, warned me against relying, as he
thought I must, upon achieving any kind of

success with my operas in Italy; it was not their *terrain,* and he expressed surprise that I myself had failed to realise this.

" I still remain the only guest (tenant) in my palace, and dwell in a spaciousness at which, at first, I was frightened. But I hardly could find anything less expensive, certainly nothing more comfortable, and so I moved into my grand salon, which is again as large as that at the Wesendonks', with passable frescoes, superb mosaic flooring and magnificent acoustics for the Erard. I at once fought a successful campaign against whatever was stiff and uncomfortable in the arrangements. The doors between an immense bed chamber and a smaller room adjoining I had lifted out and portières hung in their place, but not of such fine material as the last ones in the ' Retreat.' For the present cotton stuffs had to suffice. They suggest stage settings. They had to be red, because every-thing else was furnished in that colour; only the bed chamber is in green. A vast floor space affords me ample room for a morning promenade. One side borders on the canal, with a balcony, the other on the court in which is a well-paved garden. In these premises I pass my day until about five o'clock in the evening. My tea in the morning I brew myself. I have two cups, one of which I bought here, and out of which I allow Ritter to drink if I bring him home with me of an evening. The other, which is very large and beautiful, I use myself. I also have a fine pitcher, which I did not buy here. It is white with golden stars, which, however, I have not yet counted. Probably there are more than seven! [An allusion to the constellation of the Great Bear in Wagner's adopted coat-of-arms.]

"At five o'clock the gondolier is summoned. For I am so situated that whoever wants to call on me has to come by water (which gives me an agreeable feeling of isolation)! Through the narrow alleys, right and left, but (as you know) 'sempre dritto!' to the Piazza di San Marco and the restaurant where usually I meet Ritter. From there 'sempre dritto' in the gondola toward the Lido or the Giardino publico, where I generally walk awhile, then again in the gondola back to the Piazzetta to saunter up and down a little and take my ice in the Café de la Rotunde and then proceed to the Traghetto, which brings me back by way of the shadowy, melancholy canal to my palace, where the lighted lamp awaits me.

" The wonderful contrast between the grave and silent dignity of my abode and its situation, and the ever cheerful brilliance of the Piazza and all connected with it, the agreeably indifferent whirl of humanity, the quarrelsome gondoliers, the quiet return in the dusk and under the first shadows of night, rarely fail to leave me untouched by a grateful sense of repose. So far I have looked for no other impressions. I have not yet felt any urgent need of examining the works of art. That I am putting off until winter. At present I am glad to be able to derive satisfaction from the unvarying routine of my days.

" My lips are sealed save towards Ritter, [Julie Ritter's son] who is close-mouthed and never makes a nuisance of himself. He parts from me every evening at the Traghetto and rarely sets foot in my abode. I could not possibly have chosen a place more in keeping with my present requirements. In a small, unimportant, uninteresting locality the animal craving for social intercourse would, in the end, have been driven to seek opportunity for

its gratification, and such intercourse, growing out of such need, is the very thing sooner
or later that is bound to become distasteful,
whereas nowhere could I live in more complete
retirement than right here. For the life
about me which daily renews itself with
vividly contrasting impressions, as interesting
and fascinating as a theatrical show, does
not lure me to play an individual role therein,
for fear that my doing so would cause me
to lose my interest in the drama as an objective onlooker. And thus my existence in
Venice mirrors my attitude toward the world
in general, at least as it seems to me it should
and must be according to my own perception
and the requirements to which I am resigned.
How I am forced to regret the consequences
whenever I step out of it!

" The other evening on the Piazza di San
Marco, when the military band that plays
there on Sundays performed selections from
' Tannhäuser ' and ' Lohengrin,' it seemed to
me, in spite of the annoyance caused by the
dragging tempi, that really all this did not
concern me in the least.

" Evenings when I am on the water and look
out over the sea, which, clear and motionless

like a mirror, draws the sky down to the horizon, the rosy light of parting day so perfectly reflected in the water, that sea and sky seem joined and cannot be distinguished apart, I see in this a faithful picture of what the present holds for me. Present, past and future are as little to be distinguished from one another as over there the sea and sky. There are shadowy lines, too. These are the low islands that stand out here and there. A distant mast shows itself against the horizon. The evening star twinkles, the stars beam, up there in the heavens and down here in the sea. What is the past, what is the future? I see only the stars and the pure, rosy radiance; and in between my boat glides silently to the subdued cadence of the oar.—That may be the present.

" Greet the dear angel for me many thousand times; and let her not disdain the silent tear that courses down my cheek ! "

COMMUNINGS OF A STRICKEN SOUL

Nothing possibly could show more forcibly Wagner's total abstraction from the world than his unconcern over the indifferent performance of his own works, which he notes in this letter. I have ascertained that the band which played them was Archduke Maximilian's, who was then Governor of the Austro-Italian provinces, and later became Emperor of Mexico. Wagner was a lonely exile; Maximilian apparently the favourite of fortune. Yet compare their ultimate fates—the brilliant career which the future had in store for Wagner with the tragic death of Maximilian in Mexico!

Often while in Venice Wagner felt the pinch of poverty. Once he even was obliged to pawn the only three valuables he possessed— a silver snuff-box, which had been presented to him by the Grand Duke of Weimar; a bonbonnière, the gift of the Princess Sayn-Wittgenstein, and his watch. On December 31, 1858, his means had dwindled to about six dollars, yet, when on that evening a letter arrived from Liszt in which that composer spoke with enthusiasm of the first " Tristan " proofs recently received by him, Wagner hurried to the telegraph office and expended a considerable part of what little money he had left on a long telegram of thanks and good wishes for the new year to his friend.

RICHARD WAGNER
From a photograph especially taken for
Mathilde Wesendonk

The journals which Wagner kept in Venice
mirror his life, his thoughts—secrets of his
soul that move us profoundly as we con-
template this great genius, alone, forsaken,
going his solitary way, stealing like a shadow
amid relics of former greatness, gliding like
a spirit over the melancholy lagoons. Here
are memories; protests—" you are resigned,
calm "—heartbreaking realisations of the
present; cries of revolt against a conventional
world, " where only the most commonplace
seems bent on enjoying existence "; plaintive
notes of resignation; resolves to resume work
on " Tristan "; philosophical reflections; pre-
monitions that he and his Isolde shall meet
again, " like spirits once more drifting
toward the spot where they have suffered ";
but always—always—the communings of a
stricken soul with the one being who can bring
consolation.

" THE BLISS OF BEING LOVED BY YOU "

Venice, September 3, 1858.
Yesterday I wrote to you and to our friend.
Until now I have been occupied with my
journey, and with the arrangements here, but

from now on I propose to keep my journal
regularly. My route was over the Simplon.
The mountains, and especially the long Wallis
valley, oppressed me. I passed a beautiful
hour on the garden terrace of the Isola Bella.
A wonderfully sunny morning. I knew the
spot well and dispensed with the guidance of
the gardener, in order that I might be alone
there. A wonderful feeling of peace and exaltation came over me, so exquisite—that it
could not be of long duration. But what lifted
me out of myself, the lasting thought in me
and with me, was the bliss of being loved by
you.

I passed the night in Milan, arriving in
Venice on the 29th of August. During the
passage of the Grand Canal toward the Pia-
zetta, a touch of melancholy and sad reflections. Grandeur, beauty, decay, rubbing
elbows. Comforted by the thought that here
was no bloom of modern civilisation, therefore none of its bustling triviality.

Piazza di San Marco. Enchantment. A
bit of world, distant and extinct; in every
way congenial to my craving for solitude.
Nothing here suggests actual life. It touches
one objectively, like a work of art. Here I

desire to remain—hence shall do so.—Next day, after much hesitation, engaged lodgings on the Grand Canal, in a mighty palace, of which, at present, I am the sole tenant. Spacious, lofty chambers, through which I can roam at will. My abode being an important matter, because it houses the working machinery of my mind, I expend much care upon it, so that everything shall be arranged to my liking. I write at once for my Erard. It should sound wonderfully well in my great and lofty palace salon. The deep, peculiar silence of the canal appeals to my mood. Not until five o'clock in the evening do I leave my residence for dinner. Then a promenade toward the public gardens. A brief halt on the Piazza di San Marco. Its individual characteristics, its seething mass of humanity, are truly foreign to me and wholly unsympathetic, but serve to distract my thoughts from myself, impressing me like a scene in a theatre. Toward nine o'clock return to my palace in a gondola. Find a lamp lighted, and read a little until bedtime.

Thus my outward life will flow on, and thus it suits me. Unfortunately it is becoming known that I am here, and I have given orders once and for all that no one is to be admitted. This solitude, such as scarcely can be found elsewhere—and so readily found here, soothes me and inspires me with hope.

" MY FATE, MY DESIRE—MY LOVE "

Yes, I hope to grow strong for you! To preserve you for myself means to preserve my art for myself. With it—to live to console you, that is my aim. That chimes in with my nature, my fate, my desire—my love. Thus I am yours; thus you too shall revive for me. Here my " Tristan " shall be completed—though the whole world rage, and with " Tristan," if I may, I shall return to you, to see you, to comfort you, to bless you! That I hold out to myself as my loftiest, most sacred endeavour. Well then! Hero Tristan, heroine Isolde! Help me! Help my angel. Here ye shall bleed together. Here the wounds shall be healed, and from here the world shall learn the loftiest, noblest stress of love ecstatic, the wail of most impassioned bliss. A glorified life; and, angel, healed and clarified, you shall see me once more, your humbled friend.

90

Venice, September 5, 1858.

The past night I was restless and had long waking spells. My sweet child will not let me know how she fares? How wonderfully beautiful the canal at night. Bright stars, waning moon. A gondola glides past. In the distance gondoliers call to each other in song. This is extraordinarily beautiful and impressive. They no longer sing the stanzas of Tasso, but the melodies undoubtedly are very old, as old as Venice itself, and surely older than the Tasso stanzas which no doubt merely were adapted to them. Thus in the melodies what was genuine has been preserved, while the stanzas, like mere passing phenomena, were taken up and finally lost in them. These deeply melancholic melodies, sung with resounding, powerful intonation, borne from far across the water and dying away in the farther distance, have moved me profoundly.[1]

"I KNEW BUT THAT YOU LOVED ME"

Venice, September 8, 1858.

To-day I heard from Frau Wille. It was my first news of you. You are resigned,

[1] One of them suggested to Wagner the plaintive Shepherd lay in the third act of "Tristan."

calm, determined to carry out the resignation! Parents, children, duties.

How strange all this seemed to me in my mingled mood of hope and sorrow.

Whenever I thought of you, parents, children, duties—never entered my mind. I knew but that you loved me, and that everything in this world that strives for the sublime is destined for unhappiness. Seen from this height, it frightens me to have the cause of our sorrow pointed out to me so clearly. Suddenly I see you in your beautiful home;— see all that; hear of those by whom we ever must remain misunderstood, who, though strangers, yet are near to us and stand between us and our hearts' desires. An enraged man puts this question: " Are you to sacrifice everything to those who cannot comprehend or appreciate you, yet demand everything of you?" I can and will not see or hear of such a thing if I am to remain worthy of fulfilling my mission. Only from the depths within can I gather strength. Everything from without that seeks to strengthen our resolution only arouses me to bitterness.

You hope to see me in Rome for a few hours this winter? I fear that I shall not be able to

bear the ordeal. To see you, and then, under
the smug supervision of another, part from
you!—Could I bear that so soon?—Hardly!
And you want no letters from me?

I have written you and—surely hope not to
be rebuffed by the return of that letter. Yes,
I am sure of your reply!

Away with these foolish fancies! I hope.

Venice, September 10, 1858.

Yesterday I was quite ill with fever. In the
evening I received another letter from Frau
Wille;—in it my billet to you was—returned
unopened.

That should not have happened! Not that!

That you are recovering and growing strong
again is a comfort. I also find consolation,
a consolation that savours of revenge, in the
certainty that the time will come when you
will read the letter that has been returned
to me, and feel how greatly I have been
wronged by its return! And yet how often
I have suffered similar injustice.

" GOOD, PURE, BEAUTEOUS ONE! *"*

Venice, September 13, 1858.

I have been so depressed that I have not

cared to take even my journal into my confidence. Then, to-day, your letter came—the letter to Frau Wille. That you loved me I well knew. You are, as ever, kind, sympathetic, and thoughtful. I had to smile and almost rejoice over this, my last misfortune, since it is the cause of the exalted feeling you have inspired in me. I understand you—even in those matters in which I seem to consider you somewhat unjust,—for toward me there is injustice in everything that is palmed off as a pretext to guard you against my seeming importunity. At least I thought I had proven by the terrible experience through which I have passed in Zurich lately that I —can yield; therefore have a right to feel that to cast doubt on my spirit of resignation. and my delicacy of feeling is a deep injury. But wherefore dwell on all this? The sublime beauty of my exaltation has been marred, and now my spirit again must strive to compass the painful ascent of those heights. Forgive me, if still I stumble!—I will be cheerful again—as much so as I can. Soon I will write to Frau Wille; but even in my letters to her I will be temperate. My God! All this is so hard to bear, and yet what is best

can be won only through moderation.—Yes!
'tis well, and all shall go well again. Our love
soars over every obstacle, and every restraint
makes us richer, more spiritual, nobler, and
more and more concerned with the spirit and
essence of our love, ever more indifferent to
the unessential. Yes, good, pure, beauteous
one! we shall conquer.—Even now we are in
the full flush of victory.

Venice, September 16, 1858.

For the first time I freely breathe in this
equable, blissful, untainted air; the magical
" atmosphere " of the place casts its melancholy, yet cheerful spell over me and weaves
an ever beneficent enchantment. In the
evening when I am borne in a gondola to the
Lido, the sounds about me unite in a long
sustained, soft violin tone which I love and
with which I once compared you. Now you
can realise what my sensations are here in the
moonlight on the sea!

" I WAS BORN AGAIN "

Venice, September 18, 1858.

A year ago to-day I finished my " Tristan "
poem and took the last act to you. You led

me to the chair near the sofa, embraced me
and said:

"Now I have nothing more to live for."

That day, that hour, I was born again.—
Up to that moment I had been in the before-
life. It passed, and the after-life began. For
only in that wonderful moment did I experience life itself. You will recall how it affected
me. Not passionately, stormily, ecstatically,
but solemnly, deeply moved, permeated by a
mild and grateful warmth, emancipated as if
forever, I gazed into the future.

Ever more sadly I had been withdrawing
from the world. With me everything had become negation, declination. Even my art had
become painful to me. For it had grown to
be a longing, an unfulfilled longing for negation and renunciation—a search for that,
which, uniting itself with me, would affirm me
for its own. It was vouchsafed during that
moment, vouchsafed with such unerring certainty that a holy calm took possession of
me. A lovely woman, shy, retiring, launched
herself boldly upon a sea of suffering and
sorrow, that she might provide that glorious
moment for me, and say to me, I love you!—
And thus you consecrated yourself to death

96

that you might give me life, thus I received
your life that with you I might part from
this world, to suffer with you, to die with
you.—The dread sorcery of longing was dis-
pelled!—And this you too know, that never
since then have I been at odds with myself.
Confusion and torment might be our lot;
even you might be tempted to yield to the lure
of passion. But I—you well know it—I remained ever the same, and my love for you,
however terrible the temptation of the
moment, never could lose its fragrance, aye,
not even the most delicate atom thereof. All
that was bitter had vanished from me. I
might err concerning myself, might experience sorrow and suffering, but it always was
clear to me, that your love was the noblest
thing in my life and that without it my existence would be a contradiction.

To you gratitude, you lovely, loving angel!

"THAT DISTANCE WHICH MUST BE NEARNESS"

Venice, September 23, 1858.
The pitcher and cup have arrived. They
are a friendly token, the first from the out-

side world. What do I say? From the outside world? How can anything from you
come from the outside world? And yet—it
comes from that distance which must be near-
ness to me. A thousand thanks, sweetly in-
ventive being! Thus silently, yet how clearly,
we utter to one another words that must remain unspoken.

"DID I BRING MISFORTUNE?"

Venice, September 29, 1858.

Now the waning moon is late in rising.
When it was in its full glory it afforded me
some consolation through agreeable impressions of which I stood in need. After sunset
I regularly travelled toward it in my gondola
in the direction of the Lido. The struggle
between night and day was a wonderful spec-
tacle in the clear sky. To the right, in the
deep rosy heavens, twinkled the evening star,
serenely bright. The moon in all its splendour
threw its glittering net toward me across the
sea. Homeward bound, my back was turned
toward it. My gaze, ever wandering in the
direction where you abide and from where you
were gazing at the moon, was met, right

above the familiar constellation of the Great
Bear, gravely yet brightly, by the growing
light-trail of the comet.[2] This held no terror
for me, as nothing does any more, since I no
longer have any hope, any future. In fact
I was obliged to smile at the superstitious
fright which people show over such phenomena, and with a certain bravado I chose
it for my own constellation. I saw only
something uncommon, bright and wonderful.
Am I too a comet? Did I bring misfortune?
—Was it my fault?—I could not take my eyes
off it.

Silent and composed I arrived at the Piazzetta with its bright lights and never-spent
wave of gaiety. Then along the melancholy
canal. Right and left superb palaces. Profound silence. Only the gentle gliding of
the gondola and the swish of the oar. Arrival at the silent palace. Broad chambers
and corridors, with myself as solitary tenant.
The lamp is lighted. I take up the book,

2 Professor Harold Jacoby, of Columbia University,
N. Y., informs me that this comet was discovered by
Donati at Florence, June 2d, 1858, therefore is known
as Donati's comet, and that it was the brightest comet
of the nineteenth century.

read a little, think much. Silence everywhere.

Ah, music on the canal. A gondola with gaily coloured lights, singers, and players. More and more gondolas with listeners join it. The flotilla, barely moving, gently gliding, floats the whole width of the canal. Songs from pretty voices accompanied on passable instruments. Everything is ear. At last, almost imperceptibly, the flotilla makes the turn of the bend and vanishes still more imperceptibly. For a long while I hear the tones ennobled and beautified by the night, tones which as art do not interest me, but which here have become part of Nature. Finally all is silent again. The last sound dissolves itself into moonlight, which beams softly on, like a visible realm of music.

Now the moon has set.

"IN MY HEART I TREASURE HER SOUL"

I have not been well for a few days and have been obliged to omit my evening outing. Nothing has remained for me but my solitude and my futureless existence!

On the table before me lies a small picture.

100

It is the portrait of my father, which reached me too late for me to show it to you. It is a noble, gentle, sorrowful, yet intellectual face that appeals to me strongly. It has grown very dear to me.

Whoever enters here expects to find the picture of a dearly beloved woman. No! I have no picture of her. But in my heart I treasure her soul. Let anyone who can, see that! Good night!

"NATURE IS HEARTLESS"

Venice, September 30, 1858.
Again I have conceived a strong aversion to youthful marriages. Except among wholly commonplace persons I have not met with any such union which in due time did not prove a mistake. And then what misery! Soul, character, talent—everything, in fact, shrivels up unless new and extraordinary relations, and always highly passionate ones, are entered into. Thus everything seems to me in a most deplorable state—whatever lays claim to the slightest importance suffering and helpless; while only the most commonplace appears bent on enjoying its existence. But what does

Nature care about all this? She pursues her own blind mission, seeking nothing but self-propagation, that she may ever renew life, ever begin over again, ever spread, spread—just spread. The individual upon whom she unloads all the travail of existence is no more to her than a speck of dust in this dissemination of sex, which, so long as she clings to her theory of germination, she can replace thousandfold, aye, millionfold. Therefore I listen unwillingly if anyone appeals to Nature as his authority. With the elect it is nobly meant, but for that very reason a different interpretation is placed upon it. For Nature is heartless and unfeeling, and every egotist, aye, every savage, can appeal to Nature more securely and more understandingly than the man of keen sympathies.

What kind of marriage is that, upon which, in the enthusiasm of youth at the first prompting of sex, we enter for life? How rarely parents take counsel of their own experience. Instead, if they have managed to find refuge from their misery in a kind of tolerant indifference toward each other, they forget all about it, and allow their children to rush headlong into the same rut! There again

Nature, as everywhere, metes out to the individual misery, despair, death, leaving it to himself to rise above these only by resigning himself to the inevitable. That at least Nature cannot prevent; and then she looks on with astonishment and possibly says to herself, " Is that really what I have been trying to accomplish? "

I am not wholly well yet, but hope much from to-night if only I can count on tranquil sleep. That you surely do not grudge me? Good night!

" SPURN NOT MY PITY "

Venice, October 1, 1858.

You, my child, I no longer pity. Your journal which you lately have sent me, your latest letters, breathe a spirit so lofty, so loyal to its ideals, so purified and clarified by suffering, so master of itself and of the world, that I can only rejoice with you, honour you, worship you. No longer do you look upon your grief wholly as your own, but as part of the sorrow of the world. In fact you cannot regard it in any other light than that of the universal world-sorrow. In

the noblest sense of the word you have become a poetess.

But, ah, how I pitied you during that
moment when you had thrust me from you,
when, no longer the victim of sorrow but of
passionate desire, you thought yourself betrayed and your noblest feelings misinterpreted. At that moment you appeared to me
like an angel whose God had deserted her.
And, swiftly as your distress brought me to
my own senses, it made me equally swift in
bringing comfort and refreshment to your
perturbed spirit. I found the friend whose
privilege it has been to be consolation, inspiration, alleviation and reconciliation to
you. Behold, pity did that! Verily, I thrust
self aside, renounced forever the joy of seeing
you, of being near you, could I but know you
tranquil, cheerful, fully yourself again.
Wherefore spurn not my pity when you see
me offering it, since now my only feeling
toward you is one of rejoicing with you! Ah,
this is the highest exaltation, it can exist only
between those who are in fullest sympathy.
From common souls, upon whom I may bestow my pity, I am forced to turn quickly
as soon as they demand that I rejoice with

them. This was the ground of my last difference with my wife. She, unfortunate one, had construed in her own way my decision never again to enter your house, and interpreted it as a breach with you. Hence, on her return, she expected that, as between her and myself, all would again be agreeable and intimate. How terribly I had to undeceive her! And now, rest! Rest!—Another world opens up before us! Be blest to me in it, and doubly welcome as a sharer in our common joy!

"THE WORLD DOES NOT SEEM TO WANT ME"

Venice, October 3, 1858.

After all, my lot is pretty hard! When I pause to consider the vast amount of sorrow, impatience and torment I am obliged to undergo in order to secure now and then a little leisure for myself, I feel ashamed at my efforts to force myself upon the world, since, all things considered, the world does not seem to want me. To be always and eternally engaged in a struggle for the necessaries of life, often compelled for a long period to

105

think only of how to make a beginning, how to secure material respite for myself and what is needed for actual existence, and to be obliged for this reason to disguise my real self and appear like another person to those to whom I have to be beholden for these things—that really is revolting; and to cap the climax, I must be the very one who is so constituted that he feels the humiliation more keenly than anyone else. . . .

The shocking thing about all this is that no one—especially no man—is deeply and seriously interested in me, so that, with Schopenhauer, I begin to doubt the possibility of a real friendship, and class what goes by that name with the fables. One has no idea how little capable a " friend " is of putting himself in the situation, let alone of adapting himself to, the moods of another. But this can readily be explained. In the very nature of things such a friendship can only be an ideal, while Nature herself, this cruel creator and egoist, can, with the best disposition (if ever she can persuade herself to be well disposed), see nothing more in each individual than a medium for her own exploitation, and recognises any other individual only in so

far as he flatters her self-delusion in this respect. 'Tis thus! And yet we cling to life!
Heavens, what must that be worth for which,
in spite of this consciousness, we still hold
out!

" I LOOK UP TO YOU "

Venice, October 5, 1858.

My child, the great Buddha well knew what
he was about when he placed a strict ban
upon art. Who can realise more clearly than
I that it is this unhappy art that ever makes
return to me with all the sorrows of life and
all the contradictions of existence? Were it
not for this wonderful gift, were it not for
my dominating creative imagination, I could,
according to my guiding light, follow the
urging of my heart and become a—saint;
and as saint I could say to you, " Come,
ignore everything that would hold you back;
throw off the shackles of Nature. At this
price I will show you the open road to salvation." . . .

That I may not sink under I look up to you.
But the louder I call, " Help me, stay with
me!" the farther you seem to vanish. And
the answer that comes drifting back to me is,

" In this world, where you have taken this
burden upon yourself in order that you may
realise your ideals; in this world—she does
not belong to you! On the contrary, whatever
mocks you, whatever tortures you, whatever
eternally misinterprets you, also encompasses
her, holds her in its grasp and claims her for
its own. Then why does she rejoice in your
art? Because art belongs to the world, and
she, too—belongs to that world."

" MY SWAN SANG TO YOU FROM AFAR "

Venice, October 6, 1858.

My grand piano has just arrived, been un-
packed and set up. While it was being tuned
I reread your spring journal. The Erard
is mentioned in that. I have been profoundly
affected by its arrival. A significant cir-
cumstance is connected with this instrument.
You know how long I wished for it in vain.
When I went to Paris last January—you
know why?—it is quite remarkable that it
should have occurred to me to put forth
special efforts to secure a grand piano like
this one! I had no serious purpose in anything I did; everything was indifferent to

me; there was not even the semblance of zeal in anything I undertook. But with my visit to Mme. Erard it was different. Upon this meagre, wholly commonplace individual I expended all my enthusiasm, with the result, as I learned afterwards, that she was completely carried away. I got the instrument in a jiffy, almost as if it had been a joke. Wonderful instinct of Nature which asserts itself in each individual, according to his idiosyncrasies, merely as an impulse to provide the means of existence!

But the importance of this clever stroke soon was to become clear to me. On the 2d of May, shortly before you, too, were to leave on your " trip of diversion," and I was to be completely isolated—the long expected instrument arrived. While it was being set up the weather was disagreeable, raw and cold. I was obliged for that day to give up the hope of a glimpse of you on the terrace. The piano had not entirely been set up when —suddenly you stepped out of the billiard room upon the front balcony, seated yourself upon a chair and looked over in my direction. By this time everything was in order. I opened the window and struck the first chords.

You did not even know that the Erard had arrived.

After that I did not see you again for a month, and during that time it became clearer and more certain to me that from now on we would have to remain apart! That should have been the end with me of all desire to live. But this wonderfully soft, melancholy, and sweet instrument lured me back into the realm of music. I called it my swan that had come to bear poor Lohengrin home again! Thus I was led to begin the composition of the second " Tristan " act. Life again began to weave itself into a dreamlike existence. You returned. We did not speak, but my swan sang to you from afar.

Now I am far, far away from you. Heaven-high the Alps roll between us. It becomes clearer to me how all this must eventuate; and that life in its true meaning no longer exists for me. " Alas! " I often thought, " if my Erard only were here. That would help, and help must come! " Long, long I had to wait. Now at last it is here, this work of art with its lovely tone, which I won for myself at the time when I realised that I must lose you. How clearly the symbolism of my

110

genius, my Daimon, speaks to me from it! How unconsciously I stumbled upon this piano. But my sly instinct knew well what it was after!—The wing-shaped piano! Yes, a wing! Would it were the wing of the angel of death!

" FOR YOUR SAKE I HAVE LET IT STAND *"*

Venice, October 9, 1858.

At last I have begun.—With what?

I had only slight pencil sketches of our songs, in many cases incomplete and so indistinct that I feared they would entirely slip my memory. First of all I went to work to play them over and recall them to memory. Then I wrote them out carefully. Now it will not be necessary for you to send me your copies. I have them myself.

And so that has been my first work. With it I have tried my wings.—Anything finer than these songs I never have composed and there is very little in my works worthy of comparison with them.

"And solves your riddle!
Holy Nature."

I should like to rechristen "Holy Nature."

111

The sentiment is right enough, but not its expression, since nowhere is Nature holy save when she conquers self and abdicates. But— for your sake I have let it stand.

" THE PROTECTING, REDEEMING HAVEN "

Venice, October 12, 1858.

My mode of life up to the time when I found you, and you at last became mine, lies clearly before me. I had withdrawn more and more from my relations to the world, whose trend, so wholly opposed to mine, affected me ever more painfully and inconsolably, without it being possible for me as an artist and as a man standing in need of help, to break all ties that held me to it. I kept aloof from people because contact with them only grieved me.

Persistently I sought solitude and retirement, nourishing only, but for that reason all the more ardently, a longing in my heart that in a predestined individual I would find the protecting, redeeming haven which would welcome me freely to its refuge, and which, in the nature of things, only could be a loving woman. This, my poetically-prophetic

112

genius enabled me to comprehend even before
I had found her, for the most unselfish efforts
of men to befriend me had shown me how impossible it was that the friendship of any man
could offer me what I longed for.

Never, however, had I the slightest presentiment that I should find what I sought for so
completely, so aptly created to soothe my
longing and comfort my desires, as I found it
in you.   Once more:—That you could persuade yourself to brave all world-sorrow in
order to say to me, " I love you ! "—that has
proven my salvation, and has won for me that
blessed feeling of repose which has given to
my existence a wholly different signifi-
cance.

But this bliss has been attained only through
all possible love-grief and suffering.   We have
drained them to the dregs !—And now that we
have passed through everything, now that
nothing has been spared us, the germ of that
higher life, which we have achieved in the
pangs and suffering attendant on its birth,
manifests itself.   In you this germ lives on
so pure, so secure, that I can only let you
see, to your joy, to our mutual joy, how it is
developing in me.

113

"WE HAVE NOTHING FURTHER TO LONG FOR"

The world has been overcome. Through our love, our sorrow, it has overcome itself. It no longer is an enemy before which I flee, but an object wholly indifferent and unessential to which I can turn without fear or pain; therefore, even without any real disgust. This I realise all the more because, theoretically, my impulse to withdraw from the world no longer is as strong as formerly. Until now that impulse was the result of unstilled longing, seeking and yearning, which have now—I feel it—been assuaged. The later developments as between ourselves have made me fully conscious that we have nothing further to seek, nothing further to long for. Considering how completely you have given yourself to me, I cannot characterise my feeling as resignation, least of all as despair. This daring interpretation of my state of mind appeared to me formerly as an impossible result of my yearning quest. Now, made happy by you, I am absolved from it. A holy peace is mine. The impulse is dead because it has been satisfied.

114

This calm state of mind (the result of innumerable struggles with the world, and finally of my salvation through your love), probably will lead me eventually to settle in some spot where the means of exploiting my art will be at my disposal, something that will be a sore trouble to me (since the game no longer seems worth the candle), so that, according to my humour or caprice, I can arrange for occasional and at least tolerable performances of my works. Of course anything like a position or an appointment does not enter my mind. Moreover, I have not the least preference for one place or another, for —nowhere would I seek anything definite or individual, and least of all intimate. I am free of any such desire! On the contrary, I will grasp only at that which will enable me to maintain the most ordinary, indeed superficial, relations with my surroundings, and this may prove the easier the larger the place is. The possibility of falling back upon some intimate relationship such as I might establish in a place like Weimar, I do not for a moment consider. Such an idea is decidedly repulsive to me. I can show due regard for my deep-rooted prejudice against the world only by dealing with humanity in its totality, without any closer, individual relationship. An effort, like that in Zurich, where I sought to attract everyone toward me, I never could be capable of making again.

"AS IF IN DREAMS"

Such is the groundwork of my present disposition. How it will eventually result outwardly I cannot—as I have said—state with certainty. That, moreover, is a matter of total indifference to me. Of anything permanent regarding my future I have no thought. I am, while striving for a permanency, so accustomed to change, that I now give it full play, the more willingly the less it concerns me.

How our personal relations to one another, yours and mine, will develop—the one consideration that still affects me painfully—we, too, beloved, must leave to fate.

And herein lies the pang, the thorn of sorrow and of bitterness against others who seek to make the divine comfort of approach impossible for us, without in the least benefiting themselves thereby! Here we are not free, and depend upon those toward whom

116

with the greatest sacrifice in our hearts, we must turn in order to bestow upon them the first rites of pity. You will bring up your children—and with my blessing full upon you! May they prove a joy and a noble inspiration to you! I shall look on with profound satisfaction.—Probably we shall see each other again, but, I opine, in the near future, as if in—dreams, solitary spirits drifting toward the spot where they have suffered, that once more they may find in a look, in a pressure of the hand, the consolation that lifted them above this world and vouchsafed them a glimpse of heaven.

"AND SO, FAREWELL, MY HEAVEN!"

Should I—through the deep sense of repose that has come o'er me—be preserved to beautiful and clarified old age, I would wish that you might again be quite near me, all suffering, all jealousy allayed. The "Retreat" might then become a reality. I might even require care and nursing. Surely these would not be denied me. Then, perhaps—you would after all appear in the green workroom to take me in your arms and with the parting kiss receive my soul.—Then my journal would leave off where it began.—Yes, my child, let this journal end here! It offers you my grief, my exaltation, my struggles, my outlook upon the world, and everywhere—my abiding love for you! Accept it kindly and forgive me if anywhere it opens a wound.

And so, farewell, my heaven, my salvation, my blessed, pure, lovely woman! Farewell! In the deepest sanctuary of my heart I bless you!

THE MOAN OF A BREAKING HEART

III

WITH these wonderful introspective passages Wagner closed his first journal. The letters from Mathilde to which he refers must have been written to the faithful Brangäne (Frau Wille), and by her forwarded to him; so, too, Mathilde's journal.

He began his second journal on October 18, 1858, and the last entry is dated January 1, 1859. On January 19 he begins writing to Mathilde direct, the ban on letters evidently having been removed. His second journal is in part even more rhapsodical, more despairing, than the first. A highly dramatic passage in it shows that at one time suicide was in his thoughts. Besides great depression of mind and soul, Wagner was far from well physically, and there is a gap in the journal of over a month (November 1 to December 8) occasioned by severe illness. Nevertheless there are, in spots, glimpses of his old brave self afforded by references to his work on " Tristan."

" I shall live forever in it. And with me——"

It is easy to supply the blank; and the passage, though brief, points eloquently to the source of his inspiration.

"IT FILLS OUR SOULS FOREVER"

Venice, October 18, 1858.

A year ago we passed a beautiful day at the Willes'. . . . As we were returning from a walk toward the height your husband offered Frau Wille his arm. That left me free to offer you mine. We spoke of Calderon.[1]— What a good subterfuge he was!—Returned to the house, I seated myself at the new piano.—Even I was surprised at my beautiful playing.—It was an exquisite, all-satisfying day. Have you celebrated it to-day? —Ah, this period had to bloom for us at least once; now 'tis past. But its flower has not faded. It fills our souls forever with its fragrance.

"MY LIFE DEPENDS UPON YOU"

Venice, October 31, 1858.

Do you not realise, my child, that my life depends upon you—upon you alone? That

[1] In Zurich Wagner and Mathilde had read several of the Spanish dramatist Calderon's plays together.

the mingled cheer and seriousness with which
the journal I sent you closed, merely mir-
rored the beautiful spirit that I have caught
from you? Oh, think me not so great that
by myself and of myself I could be what I
am and as I am. I feel that most deeply
now. Unspeakable sadness and grief cleave
me to my innermost.—I receive your missive,
your journal, read your answer!—Are you
really still in ignorance that I live only
through you? Will you not believe it, though
I have assured you of it so recently? To be
like you, to be worthy of you—that is the
goal of my endeavour! Do not scold me if I
tell you that I am wholly like you, have the
same feelings with you, share your moods,
your most exquisite grief, not only because
it is yours, but also because it has become
clear to me that it is mine as well!

"ALL IS ILLUSION, DELUSION!"

Do you still remember when I was in Paris,
how we wrote to each other, and after we had
enthusiastically communicated our noble res-
olutions to each other, broke out, as if by
common impulse, into a paroxysm of grief?

So it is, and so it will ever be!—All is illusion,
delusion! We were not created to rearrange
the world according to our liking. Oh, dear,
bright angel of truth! Blessings upon you
for your heavenly love! Oh, I understand it
all! What anxious days I have passed!
What ever-growing anguish! The world
became clogged, and I could breathe only
when I felt your breath upon me.

"POOR, SAD, CAST DOWN MAN THAT I AM"

Oh, sweet, sweet woman mine! To-day,
poor, sad, cast down man that I am, I have
no consolation to offer you! I have no balsam
to give you, nor—any healing for your sorrow. How should I be able to heal your
sorrow? My tears flow freely in bitter
streams—will they make you whole?—I know
they are tears of love, such love as never was
loved before; into their stream is poured all
the sorrow of the world. Yet they give me
all the joy I would know this day; a deep and
inward certainty, an inalienable right that
cannot be torn from me. They are the tears
of my everlasting love for you. Could they

make you whole?—Heavens! more than once I was on the point of leaving here and going to you. Did I desist out of consideration for myself? No! Surely no! But out of consideration—for your children!—Therefore—once more—and always, hold fast! fast! The time is not yet ripe. It seems—it seems—to me—as if the time would come when I can meet you—in a manner more dignified, more consonant, more worthy of you; and this I would so love to do!—Yet, how weak is all endeavour!

No, no, sweet child! I know all, understand all!—I see everything with a clear vision, as clear as the sun! I am going mad!—Let me stop here! Not to seek repose, but to drown myself in the ecstasy of my grief!—Oh, lovely one!—No! No! He will not betray you.—Not—he!

"I SHALL DIE IN YOUR ARMS"

Venice, November 1, 1858.

This is All Souls' Day!

I have awakened after a brief but profound slumber, and after terrible suffering such as I never have endured. I stood on the balcony

125

and gazed down into the black flood of the canal. A storm was raging. A leap, a fall, and none would have been the wiser. Yes, a leap, and all my suffering would be at an end. Already I had my fist doubled to draw myself up to the rail. But could I—with the vision of yourself—of your children before me?

And now All Souls' Day has dawned!

All souls! Peace be with ye!

Now I know it is decreed that I shall die in your arms! Now I am sure of it! Soon I shall see you again, surely in the spring; perhaps even in the middle of winter.

For, my child, the last thorn has been drawn out of my soul! . . . I can bear all now. Soon we shall meet again!

Lay but little stress upon my art! I have realised that it offers neither consolation nor compensation; but forms only the accompaniment to my deep harmony in you, and the nourishment of my desire to die in your arms.

When the Erard came it sufficed to caress me with hope only because, after the storm, your deep, unalterable love shone for me more surely, more brightly than ever. With you

I can achieve everything;—without you, nothing! Nothing! Do not allow yourself to be deceived by the mingled mood of cheerfulness and sadness with which my last journal closed. 'Twas but the reflection of your own beautiful, grave exaltation. Everything crumbles into ruin before my very eyes, if ever I perceive the slightest spiritual disagreement between us. Trust me, only one! You hold my fate in your hands, and only with you can I perfect aught.

And so, after this terrible night, I beseech you: Have faith in me, unquestioning, infinite faith! And this means only: Be convinced that with you I can accomplish everything, without you nothing!

"CONTINUE TO LOVE ME"

Oh, believe me, believe me, you are all that is serious with me! During this past night, when I drew back my hand from the balcony rail, it was not my art that stayed me! In that dread moment the real axis of my life around which my decision to die revolved back to renewed desire to live appeared before me with almost visible certainty. It was you! You! Like a smile the thought came over me—would it not be more blessed to die in her arms?

It is hard, so hard for us, dear child! But for this very reason we are so rich that we are able to discharge every debt of life and yet reserve to ourselves its greatest treasure. But, dearest, please—you will not remain silent? And, if I cannot "make you all whole," you will at least not disdain the "balsam" I can offer?

We shall see each other soon! . . .
Farewell!
All Souls' Day!
Farewell!
And continue to love me!

"A STRANGER I SLUNK THROUGH THE CROWD"

Venice, December 8, 1858.

To-day I was able for the first time to go again into the open air, but I am not quite well yet. This last illness, during which I was quite helpless, because I was unable to move, has nevertheless, through the expe-

riences that have come to me, cleared up many
things regarding myself. Karl Ritter left
nearly three weeks ago. Accordingly there
has been no one to speak to save the physician and the servants. Strange that I should
not have felt the slightest desire for other
company.

On the contrary, when a Russian prince
whom I could not well disappoint, and who
is, besides a most intelligent person, in a
musical way, too, came to call upon me, I
really was heartily glad when he left. I
always feel that it is a useless, inconsequen-
tial effort to converse with anyone. On the
other hand I enjoy having the servants about
me. They, with all their faults and virtues,
at least are naïve. Then too, they have
tended me with more than care, with devotion. I am grateful to them. Kurwenal
appeals to me more than Melot.

In addition to this there was a complete
cessation of communication from the outside
world. The postman hardly allowed himself
to be seen at all. To-day when I reached the
Piazza in my gondola the great and brilliant
wave of humanity swept to and fro. I have
chosen a time for eating when I am sure of

being quite alone in the restaurant. A stranger, I slunk through the variegated crowd, back to my gondola, and passed along the silent canal to my solemn palace. The lamp is lighted. Everything about me is so silent, so grave. And inwardly I have the firm and unmistakable feeling that this is my life, from which I cannot withdraw without pain and self-deception. I am happy in this conviction. The servants often find me in a cheerful mood and ready to joke with them.

"WHAT MUSIC THAT IS GOING TO BE!"

Since yesterday I have been working on " Tristan " again. I still am on the second act. But—what music that is going to be! I could devote my whole life to working only on this score. How profoundly beautiful it is, and how pliantly the most sublime wonders adapt themselves to one's inspiration. I have accomplished nothing like it. My whole being is dissolved in it. I shall not ask to hear a note of it, if only I can finish it. I shall live forever in it. And with me——

" ' DREAMS ' HAUNTS IT "

Venice, December 22, 1858.

An exquisite morning, my dear child!

Three days I had been at the passage, "Whom you embraced, whom you have smiled upon," etc. There was a long check to my inspiration, and, in trying to compose the passage, I could not recall just how I had planned it. I was upset; I could not continue.—A little goblin knocked at my door and appeared to me disguised as the lovely Muse. In a moment the problem was solved. I went to the piano and wrote out the passage as rapidly as if I had it by heart. Whoever listens to it critically will discover something familiar in it. "Dreams" haunts it. But you will forgive that, dearest!—No, do not repent having loved me! It is heavenly!

" THE GRATEFUL DEW OF LOVE "

Venice, January 1, 1859.

No, do not repent those caresses with which you have adorned my barren life! Never before had I known them, those beautiful flowers blooming in the heart of purest love! What as poet I had dreamed was made

131

reality through a miracle. Upon the common clay of my earthly existence there descended gently and beneficently the grateful dew of love. Never had I hoped for it, yet now it seems as if it had fallen to my lot, after all. I have been ennobled, admitted to the highest order of knighthood. On your heart, in your eyes, through your lips—have I been exalted above this world. Every inch of me is free and ennobled. With a sacred dread of my own glory I tremble at the consciousness of having been loved by you so completely, with such rare delicacy, and yet with such exquisite chastity!—Ah, I breathe again the enchanted fragrance of those flowers which you plucked for me from your heart. They were not germs of life. Thus bloom the wonder flowers of heavenly death, of life in eternity. In olden times they scattered them over the body of the hero before it was consumed into divine ashes. Into this grave of flame and fragrance she who loved him threw herself that her ashes might mingle with his. Thus they were one! One element! Not two living beings; one divine element of eternity! Nay, repent not these flames, they burned so lustrously, so pure, so clear! No dark glow, no dust of ashes, no fearsome vapours ever sullied the bright, chaste flame, that never has burned so pure, so glorified, for anyone as for us, wherefore none other may know it.—Those caresses—they are the crown of my life, the blessed roses that sprung into bloom out of the crown of thorns, which alone once wreathed my brow. Now I am proud and happy! No wish, no desire! Joy, sublime consciousness, power and capacity for everything, to meet every storm of life! No! No! Regret them not! Regret them not!

THE CORRESPONDENCE RESUMED

Otto Wesendonk, being a sensible man, evidently concluded that Wagner and Mathilde might as well write to each other direct as to despatch letters and journals through the medium of Frau Wille, and on January 19, 1859, we find the correspondence resumed.

In one of these letters from Venice (March 2) is a remarkable passage regarding "Parsifal," in which Wagner mentions "a strange creation, a wonderfully demoniacal female (as Grail messenger)." This, of course, is Kundry, an entirely original conception with the composer. The " Parsifal " drama was not written until 1878-79. Yet twenty years before, Wagner, although in the midst of " Tristan," was developing the subject in his mind—a sufficient answer to those who have claimed that " Parsifal " was an afterthought designed merely for the purpose of giving Bayreuth a production somewhat similar to the " Passion Play " at Oberammergau.

Among the letters is one addressed to the Wesendonks' little girl, Myrrha. Purporting to be a letter of condolence on the death of her brother Guido, it advances a philosophical theory of the survival of the dead in the living—that her little brother Karl really is Guido, " only with another face." Though written to Myrrha, this letter doubltess was intended for her mother's eyes too.

Interesting also is a passage in the first letter in which Wagner states that while his other works came to him wholly from within, and without a suggestion of personal experience, " Tristan " is drawn from his own life.—It is easy to guess who the Isolde was.

While Wagner was in Venice he received

134

the first printed copies of his " Tristan "
drama. One of these he promptly sent to
Mathilde. On the fly-leaf she wrote Isolde's
lines :—

> Mir erkoren—
> Mir verloren—
> Heil und hehr
> Kuhn und feig—
> Todgeweihtes Haupt!
> Todgeweihtes Herz!
>
> (Won for me—
> Lost to me—
> Brave and bright
> Coward knight—
> Death-devoted head!
> Death-devoted heart!)

" AS IF BY MAGIC "

Venice, Janaury 19, 1859.

Thanks for the lovely fairy tale, my friend![2]
It is easy to understand how everything that
comes from you carries with it a certain
symbolic meaning. Thus yesterday your
greeting arrived at just the right hour, the
right moment. I was seated at the piano;
the same gold pen was weaving the last mesh

[2] " The Strange Bird," from " Fairy Tales and Fairy
Plays " written by Mathilde Wesendonk for her family
circle.

135

over the second act of " Tristan," and lin-
gering over the fleeting bliss of the first
meeting again of that loving couple.

My poetic creations always have been so
far in advance of my own experiences that I
may regard my moral development as almost
wholly due to them. " Flying Dutchman,"
" Tannhäuser," " Lohengrin," " Nibelung,"
Wodan,—all these were in my head before
anything in my own life had led up to them.
But you can readily comprehend in what
wonderfully close relationship I stand to
" Tristan." I confess freely, if not to the
world, at least to a consecrated soul, that
never before has a theme been so fully developed from actual life. In it the proportion
between inspiration and experience is so finely
balanced that a commonplace effort to adjust
it would only mar it.

"A THOUSAND, THOUSAND GREETINGS!"

And now I will keep right on complaining.
—My dwelling is large and beautiful, but
frightfully cold. I have frozen before—
that I know—but only in Italy, never in the
villa Wesendonk, and least of all in the

136

" Retreat." Never in my life have I been on a footing of such intimacy with the stove as in lovely Venice.

A wonderful sadness and longing come over me when, in very clear weather, I see from the public gardens the Tyrolese Alps in the farthest distance. At such times a dream of my youth comes over me and draws me toward the mountain summit where the fairy tale has conjured the stately palace and the lovely princess therein. 'Tis the rock on which Siegfried found his sleeping Brünnhilde. The long, smooth plain that surrounds me here, what is it but a symbol of resignation.

Ah! you come to my aid so graciously; and, when you do not, I aid myself through you.

Would you like to know how I accomplish this? I heave a deep sigh until I begin to smile. Then a rare book—or to work. Then all vanishes, for you are near me and I am with you.—If you will opportunely send me some book that you have read, I will accept it with the deepest gratitude. I read, indeed, very little. But, when I do, I read thoroughly, and you will hear from it every time.

There, where lies my crown of thorns, there too my roses, never fading, give forth their fragrance. The laurel has no charm for me, —and if I am to crown myself before the world let it be with the palm!
Peace! Peace be with us!
A thousand, thousand greetings!

"I WOULD KNOW MY FATE"

Venice, February 22, 1859.

According to the law of the gloriously perfected Buddha the penitent confesses aloud and in the presence of the whole congregation. You know how I become a Buddhist in spite of myself. Unconsciously, too, I always have believed in the Buddhistic beggar maxim. A grand maxim it is too. The devotee goes out into the cities and upon the streets of men, and shows himself naked and in penury, and by his very appearance affords believers the opportunity of performing a noble and deserving office in ministering to his needs. His acceptance of them is a bestowal of visible grace wherein the givers are blessed. He had no need of what they gave, for he had voluntarily given up every-

138

thing only that he might refresh these souls through the acceptance of their charities.

I would know my fate to the minutest details. Not to circumvent it, but to stand undeceived by it. For my future I have no need. My greatest need—you well know—I must put aside. How could I be flattered into satisfaction with any other disposition of fate? My hopes centre only on others; should such hopes prove incapable of fulfilment I will have learned how to resign them also. For in all finality each one's blessing comes to him from his own inner self. Medicine is humbug.

Does this sound serious and sad? And yet I say it to console you. I know your need of consolation, because you need to be reassured regarding myself. And now we will strive in the sweet exercise of mutually consoling each other.

"NEVER UNTIL TOO LATE DOES THE WORLD BECOME INTELLIGENT"

Germany I renounce with a calm, cold heart, for I know that I must. For the future I have decided nothing,—save—that I must complete " Tristan "!

Some day of course the world will wonder that I, of all men, should have been forced to convert my works into articles of commerce. Never until too late does the world become somewhat intelligent, and even then forgets in its childish self-deception that it still is the same senseless, heartless world. But so it is, and we cannot change it. You have passed the same comment on people in general. In fact, I remain about the same too.

I still have my little weaknesses, enjoy a pleasant dwelling, am fond of carpets and pretty furniture and, when at home and at work, take pleasure in wearing silk and velvet, and—for that reason have to write letters!

If only " Tristan " will turn out well; and he will, as never another!—Is my little hobgoblin reassured by that and my friend consoled?

" MY GOOD ANGEL BECKONS ME "

Venice, March 2, 1859.

I am in good humour over my success with the second act. Last night, Ritter and

Winterberger[3] persuaded me to play some of the principal passages. Well, that was a nice thing to do! All my other works, poor things, were thrown aside for this one act! Thus I rage against myself and ever am murdering my own offspring, save the last.

Good heavens! You know what I seek! It is transparently clear to you when you hold the crystal ball above me!

Friend, how hard it is for me, oh,—how hard! But my good angel beckons me now and then. She consoles me and gives me peace, and always when I need her most. Therefore I thank her and say to myself, " These things had to happen in order—that this might be! "

Only he who has borne the crown of thorns appreciates the palm which lies so tenderly in the hand or hovers so lightly above it, and spreads overhead like the most buoyant of angel pinions gently fanning the air and gratefully cooling it for us!

I had a visit from a Prince Dolgouroki, an amiable, thoroughly cultured and intelligent person. I was glad when he came, and even

3 Alexander Winterberger, a pupil of Liszt's.

gladder when he went. I am more contented when I am not entertained or disturbed.

" ' PARZIVAL ' HAS OCCUPIED ME MUCH "

Then too I have dipped much into philosophy, and have arrived at important results which supplement and rectify my friend Schopenhauer. But things like these I prefer to evolve in my mind rather than write them out. On the other hand poetical projects have engaged my attention in the liveliest manner. " Parzival " has occupied me much, especially a strange creation, a wonderfully demoniacal female (as Grail messenger) that assumes shape ever more vividly and convincingly in my mind. If ever I carry out this poetic conception I surely shall have accomplished something highly original. Only I do not quite know how long I shall have to live if I am to carry out all my plans. If I took much pleasure in life I might assure myself a long existence through these many projects. But that does not necessarily follow.—Humboldt tells us that Kant had intended to develop a mass of ideas in detail, but at his age was quite naturally prevented from doing so by death.

I perceive in this a possible fatalistic obstacle to the completion of " Tristan," which, however, does not move me to work more rapidly on it. Quite the contrary. I am composing it as leisurely as if I had nothing else to do for the rest of my life. For this reason it will turn out to be more beautiful than anything I ever have done; the shortest phrase signifies as much to me as a whole act. I work it out so carefully. And as I chance to be referring to " Tristan," let me tell you that I take pleasure in making you a gift of one of the first printed copies of the poem which I myself only just have received.

"THITHER WHERE THE LIGHT
GROWS DIM "

As I still am under the weather, without being really ill, I decided the other day to take a little outing in the country. My intention was to go to Vicenza, but the train went in another direction and so I arrived at Treviso. After a wretched night I started at sunrise for a good tramp of about fifteen miles.

Passing through the gate I walked straight

toward the Alps, which in their beauty and
pride resembled a huge chain that would
bar my path. It gave me much to think
about. Tired out, I returned in the evening
to the city of the lagoons and asked myself
what was the chief impression this outing on
firm soil had made upon me. I was so depressed that all I could remember was the
dust and the wretched, cruelly tormented
horses, which I saw again. Sadly I gazed
upon my silent canal. " Dust " and " poor,
tormented, miserable horses "—well, they are
not here?—but they exist.—With that I
extinguished my lamp, prayed my angel to
bless me,—with that the light within me went
out,—dust and torment vanished.

Next day to work again.

And then I had letters to write. But I
have told you about that. To-morrow I plan
more work. This letter, however, had to be
written first. With it I glide into the beyond, thither where the light grows dim,
where dust and torment vanish.

To you, child, thanks,—for being my
guide. Who would grudge it me?

A thousand greetings! A thousand rarely
beautiful greetings!

MYRRHA WESENDONK
(Afterwards Von Bissing)

MOAN OF A BREAKING HEART

Venice, March 10, 1859.

That really was a wonderfully well written letter I have received from you! Whoever doubts this should take a look at it himself! My dear child, I myself cannot write so beautifully; I am much too old for anything of the kind! Therefore, if there is anything in my reply which you are unable to decipher, ask your mother, who has been so successful in teaching you how to write, to help you read it. No doubt there are many things which you can read without mother's help. That I do not doubt for a moment. But a letter of mine is something quite different and far more difficult, for the very reason that I never had a Myrrha to instruct in writing. That is the reason I have formed a habit of writing quite in my own way and which will not be easy for you to make out. But let mother help you.

I was glad to hear from you that Karl is growing so finely. Just because he doesn't happen to have the same features as dear Guido, don't let that deter you from believing that he really is Guido, after all. Believe

me, he is quite the same Guido over again—
only with a different face. Because he happens to have different features he may grow
up to regard the world from a different point
of view than Guido's would have been. But
that will be the only difference, and, after
all, it is not as important as people seem to
think, even if it leads to a little confusion
because people see each other with different
faces, and therefore believe themselves different and each the right one. That, however,
won't last, and, when it comes to the main
point, weeping or laughing, any of us can
weep or laugh as well with his face as
another's, and if we die, as may happen
too, we may all be glad, if we have as handsome a face as your father writes me dear
Guido had. Therefore, be assured that Karl
is Guido. The latter merely wanted to bring
his features into that state of blissful repose
which most people are able to acquire only
after much weeping and laughing and other
facial distortions. In the end we all acquire
it, especially if we have been thoroughly kind
and cheerful. Karl wants to have his due
share of weeping and laughing, he has undertaken that for Guido, and for that reason he

has different features. I wish for him with all my heart that he will use them to laugh with, for the tears will come of themselves anyhow, and the ability to laugh heartily will help over many obstacles. Take my word for that!

AN INTERMEZZO AT LUCERNE

IV

WAGNER had intended to remain in Venice
until the summer. Instead, however, he left
there in March and went to Lucerne. Several
of his biographers have stated that the
activity of the Saxon authorities in en-
deavouring to secure his extradition led him
to seek refuge once more in Switzerland. In
point of fact, however, Archduke Maximilian
pigeon-holed the Saxon papers.

It appears rather that Wagner, when Guido
died, wrote a touching letter of sympathy to
Otto, which caused the latter to relent toward
the composer and to consent to his taking up
his residence, if not in Zurich, at least in some
spot reasonably convenient to that place.
Moreover, the thought that, when Wagner
had asked, " Whither I go, wilt thou, Isolde,
follow?" Isolde had elected to remain behind must have proved somewhat mollifying
to King Mark.

On his way to Lucerne Wagner stopped over

at Milan, from where he sent Mathilde a highly poetic letter. Once in Lucerne, he was not long in seeing the Wesendonks again. His impressions of his first meeting with Mathilde after such a long lapse of time he noted in his journal, where it forms the last entry. The letters which followed are noticeably less pessimistic in tone than those from Venice. Though he did not set foot in the " Retreat," and was not restored to the old-time intimacy and familiarity with the family, he visited the villa on the Green Hill, and in every way his position was less deplorable than it had been in Italy.

"A SCENE WITNESSED IN YOUR GARDEN"

Milan, March 25, 1859.

A few nights before I left I had a wonderfully sweet dream, so beautiful that I must tell you about it, although it really was too beautiful for description. So much of it as I may venture to describe was about as follows: A scene I witnessed in your garden (which, however, did not seem quite the same). Two doves flew over the mountain. I had despatched them to announce my arrival. There were two doves; why two? That I cannot explain. The two flew close together, as mates. As soon as you saw them you rose in the air to meet them. A huge, bushy laurel wreath swung in your hand, and with it you caught the pair of doves and drew them, fluttering, after you, playfully waving the wreath with the captives hither and thither. Suddenly, like the sun breaking through the clouds after a thunderstorm, there fell upon you such a blinding light that I was awakened by it.—Now you may say what you will, that was what I dreamed, except that it was infinitely more beautiful and enchanting than I can describe it. My poor brain surely could not have invented anything like it!

"SOMETHING TREMBLED DEEP WITHIN ME"

Lucerne, April 4, 1859.

And so we have dreamed the dream of meeting again, and have met. After all, was it not but a dream? Wherein lay the difference between the hours I have passed in your house and that other dream which vouchsafed

me a gracious vision of my return? I see it
almost more distinctly than the serious, sad,
longing vision that persistently declines a
niche in my memory. I have a feeling as if
I really had not seen you quite distinctly. Between us hung a heavy mist which the sound
of our voices barely penetrated. I feel as if
you, too, had not seen me, as if, instead of
myself, a spirit had entered your house. Did
you recognise me?—Heavens! I recognise it.
'Tis the road to salvation! Life, reality, ever
more dreamlike; the feelings dulled; the eye
—wide open—no longer sees; the ear gladly
misses the sound of the present. Where we
meet we do not see each other; only where we
are not our glances meet. Thus the present
no longer exists for us, and our future is
nought.—Is my work really worth so much
that I should strive to keep alive for
it?—But you?—Your children?—Are we
alive!

Then as I perceived in your face the traces
of deep suffering, as I pressed your emaciated
hand to my lips—something trembled deep
within me and a voice summoned me to a
noble duty. The wondrous power of our love
has helped us thus far; has strengthened me

and made it possible for me to see you again; has taught me this dreamlike unreality of the present, in order that I might be near you and yet unmoved; has banished ill-will and bitterness, so that I could kiss the threshold over which I am permitted to pass into your presence. And I trust this power. It will teach me to see you even through the veil which—we penitents—have thrown over ourselves, and to show myself to you in a clear, true light!

Heavenly saint, rely on me!

I shall compass it!

AFRAID "TRISTAN" WILL DRIVE PEOPLE CRAZY

Lucerne [undated, probably April 10-15, 1859.]

Child! This "Tristan" is getting to be something terrible!

This last act!

I am afraid the opera will be suppressed—provided the whole thing is not turned into a parody by bad performances; only mediocre performances can save me! Perfect ones would drive people crazy. I cannot imagine

any other result. Things have come to such
a pass as this with me! Alas!
I have been in full swing!
Adieu!

Lucerne, April 15, 1859.

If Wesendonk should not have returned, let
me know at once by telegraph. If I do not
hear from you during the morning, and this
bad weather continues, I will telegraph him
and ask him, if it is not too much trouble,
to have the coupé meet me at the railroad
station. Then we will see how we can manage
to get rid of this bad weather together on
Sunday. Is that agreeable?

CONCERNING BEDSPREADS

Lucerne, April 26, 1859.

Now there is another thing, but for heaven's
sake don't let Wesendonk know about it.—I
am accustomed always to take my own bed-
spreads and mattresses along with me—
pampered creature that I am!—The silk
covers have become so terribly dirty that I
am ashamed to have the chambermaid see
them. Could you opportunely find some
material for me in Zurich? They were green,

but, if necessary, could change to red, like the autumnal foliage.

ZWIEBACK AND A DRESSING GOWN

Lucerne, May 9, 1859.

With the arrival of the zwieback I at once became aware of what had been the matter with me. The local zwieback is too sour to inspire anything reasonable. But the sweet zwieback, to which I am accustomed from formerly, dipped in milk, at once set everything going the right way. And so I threw elaboration aside, and went on with composition, beginning with the reference to the " distant comforter." Now I am happy. The transition has succeeded beyond all expectation with a wonderful blending of two themes. Heavens, how much one can accomplish with the right kind of zwieback! Zwieback! Zwieback! thou art the medicine for distressed composers,—but it must be of the right kind! Now I have an ample supply of it; as soon as you have reason to think that it must be giving out, be sure to replenish it. I note that it is an important remedy for composers in the dumps.

Nothing has occurred. While you have allowed yourself to be interned " vers les Wille's," I have been amusing myself from my balcony with the people of Lucerne, who, with genuine fanaticism, make the most of the advantage they have over you, in being able every day to admire my new dressing gown. It must be simply stunning.

Lucerne, June 3, 1859.

Friend! I do not think that I can possibly find it agreeable to meet you next Sunday at the Willes', therefore I enclose a few lines excusing myself to Madame Wille and dated from Kissingen. I suffer so at times from the cowardice of my friends, that I almost think it is better not to rely on friends at all—at least not until the ability to deceive one's self again manifests itself and makes it possible to believe that the whole world seems to contain nothing but dear friends. That feeling is sure to return! Until then, my regards to the Wille household.

Loving thanks for the lovelier letter! More about it verbally.

Heartfelt greetings to all at home.

AN INTERMEZZO AT LUCERNE

"THE DEVIL OF A FELLOW"

Lucerne, June 5, 1859.

Child! Child! Dear child! Here is a terrible story. The master has done well again!

I have just finished playing over to myself the completed first half of my act, and I had to say to myself what the Almighty said, as he looked about Him and remarked that all was good!

I had no one to praise me, just as was the case with Him—about six thousand years ago—and so I said to myself among other things, " Richard, you are the devil of a fellow! "

HUMOURS OF EQUITATION

Lucerne, June 17, 1859.

A few hasty lines before dinner and after work. My best thanks for the ornament you have mended. I have just gotten off the first manuscript instalment of the third act to Leipzig.

Something old—it is raining.

Something new—since three days ago I have been riding.

Riding! I go out every morning. My doctor insisted on it. I am expecting fine results from it.

But do not say anything about it to Wesendonk, otherwise he will seal up all his horses should I go to Zurich.

AS TO SHAKESPEARE

Lucerne, June 21, 1859.

I have grown passionately fond of horseback riding . . . and could keep on writing about it at much greater length. But I must guard myself against becoming too passionately attached to horses, otherwise I shall again have to learn to give up something I have set my heart on.

And I have given up so many things in the course of my life—and, after all, the Wandering Jew is not allowed a horse.

I had to laugh over a line from Shakespeare, which brought me again to one of my favourite themes, intercourse with great minds, which, after all, is the best thing to lift us above the troubles of the world. This wonderfully witty smile of Shakespeare's! This divine contempt for everything worldly—

160

really it is the greatest height to which man can swing himself up from misery. Genius cannot accomplish anything greater. Only a saint could! And he no longer would have any use for wit.

A CORPUS CHRISTI PROCESSION

Lucerne, June 23, 1859.

This morning the Almighty was bustling about the streets here. It was Corpus Christi, and the whole town, led by the priests, who had put on gold dressing gowns, held procession past the empty houses. Nevertheless the passage of the Capuchin monks affected me deeply—in the midst of this unspeakably distasteful, tinselled religious comedy, a touch of melancholy. It was fortunate that I did not watch them from too near by, although I have observed several simple, honest physiognomies among the local Capuchin monks. Futhermore, I am always deeply impressed by the crucifix. Yesterday evening when these sly fellows had concluded from the direction of the wind that we would have fine weather to-day, they gathered the children into the churches, to pray for it, so that, after all, this wonderful, cloudless morning was only part of the comedy. Nevertheless I enjoyed it, and well knew that the weather really was made for me;—also who had brought it about. My best thanks!

" FRAGRANCE OF ROSES, AND FAREWELL "

Lucerne, July 1, 1859.

I once told you something about the East Indian women who threw themselves into the fragrant sea of flames. Extraordinary, how odours can recall the past. A short time ago, while I was out walking, I suddenly perceived a strong fragrance of roses. There was a little garden beside the road and the roses there were in full bloom. They recalled to me the last days in the " Retreat." Never have I loved roses as much as I did then. Every morning I plucked one and placed it in a glass on my work table. I knew that I was taking leave of the garden. This fragrance of roses to-day wove itself into this memory; sultriness, the summer sun, fragrance of roses and—farewell. Such was the mood in which I once sketched out the music of the second act.

162

AN INTERMEZZO AT LUCERNE

" MINE IS SHE EVER "

Lucerne, July 9, 1859.

I know nothing at all about what is going on in the world! Nobody takes the slightest interest in me, and I am beginning to find the situation rather agreeable. Heavens, how many things one can dispense with! The only thing I miss is your companionship, my child, for I know of no one to whom I would so love to communicate my ideas. With men that isn't possible, for even if they are friends they always are on their guard lest they should lose their identity, and are always concerned to maintain their personal opinion, therefore allow themselves to be influenced as little as possible. That is quite natural—man lives for himself. But when I stop to consider how much that is good you have lured out of me, I can only rejoice that, although you never went to work with any set purpose, you always succeeded in drawing from me what was best. How I did enjoy myself when a short time ago I introduced you to Sebastian Bach! Never before had I myself experienced so

163

much exaltation from him, and never felt myself so close to him. But I never think of
anything like this when I am alone. When
Liszt and myself made music it was something
quite different. That simply was music;
and technique and art in general played
their great roles. . . .

It is a fine thing that my bodily needs seem
to grow less and less. I am living almost
entirely on air, and my heart bleeds every time
I am obliged to pay my landlord for board,
as if I were maintaining an English appetite.

I also am able to derive pleasure from what
is really cheerful. Just think of it, lately
when I was working out the joyous shepherd
melody which is heard when Isolde's ship
heaves in sight, I gave the air a sudden turn
which was more jubilant, almost heroically
jubilant, and yet quite in folk tone. I was
on the point of completely changing everything when I suddenly became aware that the
melody did not belong at all to Tristan's
shepherd, but to none other than Siegfried.

At once I looked up the last lines of the
Siegfried-Brünnhilde scene and recognised
that my melody went with the words:

"Mine is she ever,
Forever mine
Own and owner,
My all in all," etc.

It will turn out incredibly bold and jubilant.
And so I found myself suddenly in the midst
of "Siegfried." Ought I not to gain new
confidence in life—in my capacity for endurance?

SOLFERINO AND "TRISTAN"

Lucerne, July —, 1859.

Things cannot have gone worse at Solferino
than with my work. While there the blood-
shed has ceased, I continue the terrible havoc.
To-day I killed off Melot and Kurwenal. Come
quickly if you want to look over the battle-
field before they are all buried. Thousand
greetings!

Lucerne, July 24, 1859. Evening.

I have read the beautiful fairy tale to my
Erard, which shows through its doubly beautiful tones that it comprehends everything. On
the same day you must have received my
sketches. Fair exchange! I am so passion-

165

ately taken up with my work that I regard it as a moral victory over myself when I break away from it and give up a page for a day. What will be my feelings when it is all finished! I still have about thirty-five pages of the score to compose. I think this will occupy me about twelve days. Then what will happen to me? I think that at first I will feel somewhat exhausted. Even to-day I am a little dizzy. And how I do depend upon the weather! If the air is clear and bracing I am amenable to everything, especially if one is nice to me; if, on the other hand, the atmosphere is oppressive I can bid it defiance, but it is difficult for me then to achieve anything really beautiful.

"I AM THE MADDEST CREATURE IMAGINABLE"

Lucerne, August 24, 1859.

But, child, what are you thinking of to regard me as a sage, or even to wish I were one? Why, I am the maddest creature imaginable. From the standpoint of a sage I must appear like a criminal, and for the very reason that I know so much and on such a variety of subjects, and especially because I am aware what a desirable and admirable thing wisdom is. But that puts me in just the right humour to lift myself over abysses which a sage would not even notice. For that very reason I am a poet and—what is far worse—a musician. Now think how my music, with its subtle, mysteriously flowing rills, penetrates the finest pores of sensitiveness to the very marrow of life, in order that there it may overpower whatever there is of wisdom and carefully wrought out endurance, sweep aside everything that belongs to the illusion of personal self, evoking only the wonderfully deep sighs and confessions of impotence:—how can I be a sage, who feel myself wholly at home only amid such freaks of madness?

VICISSITUDES IN PARIS

V

THE proximity of Lucerne to Zurich and the
Green Hill may have been agreeable to Wagner; on the other hand it is conceivable that
it may have been simply aggravating—" so
near and yet so far." Moreover, there was
no opportunity of producing his works in
Lucerne. Whatever indifference Wagner
may have assumed at times on this point, the
genius who creates for the stage needs the
stimulus of occasionally seeing and hearing
his own productions. The composer of
" Tristan " had nothing so much at heart as
to see that work produced,—he would offer his
life as a sacrifice, he wrote Mathilde,—and
in the autumn of 1859 he went to Paris,
secretly hoping that something might be done
there toward placing his music drama on the
stage. He remained in Paris nearly two
years, and, although he did not succeed in
producing " Tristan," events so shaped themselves that he became the musical lion of the
French capital.

171

Money for the trip and for at least part of the sojourn came from Wesendonk, who, on August 24, offered to make Wagner a loan. The composer at first declined it, because he was in negotiations with Breitkopf and Härtel for the sale of the " Nibelung " rights. Four days later he learned that the matter had fallen through, whereupon he applied to Wesendonk for an advance of the amount he had expected from the publishers, making over to him as security the publishing rights and handing him the completed " Rheingold " and " Walküre " scores. Otto's liberality did not stop here. During the second year of his stay in Paris the composer was taken seriously ill and threatened with brain fever. His wife rejoined him temporarily and nursed him. Afterwards when he desired to send her to Soden for the cure, Mathilde's husband promptly supplied him with the means. While on this subject, it might be well to add here that Wesendonk again helped him out with a loan in 1862, when the Schotts of Mayence, who were publishing his " Meistersinger," refused him further advances; and that, in 1870, when Wagner asked him to present the manuscript score of " Die Walküre," written with the American gold pen, to Louis II. of Bavaria, Otto did so and received from the king an autograph letter of thanks.

When Wagner went to Paris there was already in that city a small band of enthusiasts with whom the study of his scores was a passion, in spite of the fact that there practically were no public performances of his music. The composer appears to have known nothing of these admirers. He was greatly surprised when, on thanking a customs official, who had been untiring in his efforts to aid him in passing the furniture he had brought with him, this official replied that he was only too glad to have been of service to so great a musical genius.

The young man turned out to be Edmond Roche, the poet, who became the translator of " Tannhäuser," and who died of a broken heart soon after the failure of that work at the Opera. In a preface to Roche's collected poems written by Sardou, the latter relates the customs house anecdote, the truth of which now is borne out by Wagner's own reference to it in one of his Paris letters to Mathilde.

These letters contain interesting character sketches of the admiring circle which Wagner

173

drew around him, or rather which insisted on being drawn around him. They touch upon Berlioz, who was " devoured by envy "; Gounod, " agreeable, but hardly of very great talent," a sufficiently amusing qualification, considering his subsequent fame as the composer of " Faust " and " Romeo and Juliet " ; Gustave Doré and many others. Mention also is made of Rossini, " the old epicure," who was reported to have served one of Wagner's admirers with fish without sauce as symbolising harmony without melody, but who publicly denied any enmity toward Wagner.

In order to attract attention, Wagner (assisted by Bülow) gave three concerts at the Theatre Ventadour, January 25, 1859, and February 1 and 8, 1860. To make up for the deficit which resulted, he repeated them in Brussels, with the mortification of adding to the deficit, which, however, was met by his friend, Countess Kalergis, a niece of the Russian statesman, Nesselrode. The concerts were, however, much talked about, and finally through the efforts of Princess Pauline Metternich, wife of the Austrian Ambassador, and an intimate friend of Empress Eugenie,

Napoleon ordered that "Tannhäuser" be produced regardless of expense and under Wagner's supervision at the Opera. As is well known, the production, which was made on March 13, 1861, was a failure, owing to the opposition of the members of the Jockey Club, who were enraged because Wagner declined to introduce a ballet into the second act. After two more performances the composer himself withdrew the work, in spite of the fact that the receipts promised an unusually brilliant financial success. Wagner deemed it an insult to art to allow performances to proceed amid such a hubbub that it was almost impossible to hear what was going on on the stage.

His letters to Mathilde give what is unquestionably the most vivid picture of this period of his life—the whirl of activity into which he threw himself in preparing for the concerts and for the opera, the reaction and the depression of spirits which resulted from failure; his illness, his financial straits and the manner in which his money troubles hampered his freedom to think of work. Then there is a subtle dissertation on French musical taste, an outline of much of the first act

of " Parsifal " (remember this was years before the subject was worked out by him), and
an explanation of the reasons which governed
him in rewriting the Venusberg scene in
" Tannhäuser." These reasons are set forth
at length, but I shall do no more than refer
to them in this place, since the Paris version
long has been accepted here as final.

During this Paris sojourn Wagner made
several trips. One of these was to Baden
Baden to present his thanks to the Princess
of Prussia, who had obtained permission for
him to re-enter Germany, except Saxony,
which later also raised the ban; another to
Vienna, where for the first time he heard a
performance of his " Lohengrin "—thirteen
years after he had composed it ! He returned
from Vienna to Paris to settle up some affairs
there, and then again went to the Austrian
capital, where hopes of producing " Tristan "
had been held out to him. From Vienna he
took a trip to Venice, where the Wesendonks
chanced to be, and the meeting awakened
many sad memories. When, after his return
to Vienna, he found, while looking over one
of his portfolios, the pencil sketch of
" Dreams," from which he had developed

the great love duet in " Tristan," he wrote to Mathilde:

" Heaven knows this song pleases me more than the proud scene itself! It is more beautiful than anything else I have created! "

Again, writing from Paris, December 21, 1861, he exclaims, " That I should have composed ' Tristan ' I owe to you,"—which is, perhaps, the most significant sentence in the whole correspondence. In the same letter is a reference to " Die Meistersinger," showing that that work was beginning to take shape in his mind. Though the fact is not stated in the correspondence, it seems that during his visit to the Wesendonks in Venice, when he was downcast over the poor outlook for producing " Tristan," Mathilde reminded him of the " Meistersinger " sketch which he had presented to her in Zurich. He at once asked her to send it to him. Curiously enough, when he received it he wrote her that it contained little that was of value to him. But on comparing the sketch (which has been published in a German musical periodical) with the completed drama, it will be found to contain the germs of some of the finest scenes.

177

TRANSLATING " TANNHAUSER "

Paris, September 23, 1859.
Friend! Only these last years of my life
have ripened me into real manhood. I now
feel myself in full harmony with my own
self, and whenever truth is at stake I am sure
of myself and at one with my own will. As
regards life in general I allow myself to be
guided by my instinct. Fate has designed
for me something that is higher than the
worth of my own personality. The consciousness of this has become so much a part
of myself that I rarely question, and then
only with a smile, whether I shall do a certain
thing or not. The wonderful genius which
for the rest of this life will serve me, looks
after that, and that genius desires that I
shall accomplish whatever I can. Therefore
everything within me is perfect peace.

The ripples on the surface do not stir my
depths. I am—what I may be! Thank you,
friend.

Now I sit every morning with my young
poet and go over " Tannhäuser " with him
line for line, word for word, syllable for syllable; often strive with him by the hour to

hit on the best word; sing a passage for him and thus give him insight into a world which up to now has been entirely hidden from his view.

I take pleasure in his zeal, his growing enthusiasm, his frank confession of his former blindness—and—we shall see! At least, I know that I am caring for the future of my child as best I can!

"ONLY THERE CAN SIEGFRIED AWAKEN BRÜNNHILDE"

Paris, September 24, 1859.

As regards my material circumstances, things are turning out quite tolerably. In that respect I am advancing, and lately it seems as if I were advancing quite rapidly and as though it depended entirely upon myself how soon I can make my fortune in Paris—at least since my conversation yesterday with the Director of the Theatre Lyrique (really an agreeable and very decent fellow). Now may everything come to my aid so that all may go well this winter in order that in the spring I may be able to return to my beloved Switzerland again. For only there can Siegfried awaken Brünnhilde! That hardly could happen in Paris.

"A SURPRISING ADVENTURE"

Paris, October 10, 1859.

To-day I had a surprising adventure. I inquired in the customs house after my things that had arrived from Lucerne. The entries were in the books, but not my name. I showed my passport and gave my name, whereupon one of the officials arose and said: " Je connais bien M. Richard Wagner, puisque j'ai son medallion suspendu sur mon piano et je suis son plus ardent admirateur." " Quoi? " " Ne soyez pas surprise de recontrer a la douane de Paris un homme capable de gouter les incomparables beautes de vos partitions, que j'ai étudiées toutes." I was like one in a dream. An enthusiast in the customs house and at the moment when I had expected to meet with so much difficulty in getting my furniture!

The good fellow jumped up, ran about, and helped me. He insisted that he would have to visit me in order to pay his respects to me. He has a wife who plays the piano very well. He aspires to be literary and helps out his income through his official position. He told me about quite a wide circle here which had been formed through the growing acquaintance with my works.

People here play portions of " Tannhäuser " and " Lohengrin " for me, although unable to understand a word of the text. That they do not understand German does not appear to bother them in the least. Moreover, the Director of the Theatre Lyrique announced that he was coming for a repetition of " Tannhäuser " by myself. They all met and I was obliged to give them a careful explanation of the text in French. (You can imagine the effort!) Then to sing and play! But it seemed to open their eyes and to make a remarkable impression. Never have I had such an experience as I am having with these Frenchmen.

A MEETING WITH BERLIOZ

Paris, October 21, 1859.

DEAR CHILD: Since last All Souls' night the master has again looked upon death, but this time as a friendly comforter.

Not long ago I looked up Berlioz. I found

him just as was coming home, and in a wretched state of health. He had been taking electrical treatment as a last resort for his frightful nervous condition. He described his sufferings to me, which, beginning on his awakening, ever become worse. I recognised my own condition, and the causes which develop a similar condition in a most exaggerated manner, among which I count the nervous exertions connected with conducting, and other emotional experiences, which are wholly unknown to ordinary people. I felt that my condition would become even worse than Berlioz's if it were not that I expose myself to such exertions only very rarely, for I feel that now their effect upon me would be even more ruinous. With Berlioz, his digestion is already partially affected and— trivial as it may sound—Schopenhauer is right, after all, when he demands among other necessary physiological needs of genius a good digestion. Through my own extraordinary abstemiousness I at least can claim this serviceable requisite.

But I saw in Berlioz's suffering what probably was destined for me, and I left the poor fellow with a feeling of dread.

"YOU WILL LIVE TO FULFIL YOUR MISSION !"

Paris, November 11, 1859.

I too, am slowly convalescing and—I will confess it now—from a severe illness. Ten years ago—and in Paris—I had a bad attack of rheumatism, and the doctor insistently advised me to make every effort to prevent the attacks from reaching the heart. And now all the sorrows of my life seem to accumulate and threaten to culminate in my heart.

This time I thought that I really would succumb, but once more all this is to be driven out and I will endeavour through some nobly diverting activity to relieve the pressure at the heart. Help me in this, will you not, my friends?

"TRISTAN" PROOFS

The first good news came through myself. The proofs of the third act of "Tristan" arrived unexpectedly. You can feel with me how greatly a look into this, my most lately completed work, revived, strengthened, thrilled and inspired me. Such joy hardly

183

could come over a father even at the sight of his child. Through a flood of tears—why deny the weakness?—a voice called to me: "No, the end is not yet. You will live to fulfil your mission! He who has created such a work is still full to overflowing!

And so be it!

Then I had a sad task of love to perform. I suddenly received news of the fatal illness of my dear, fatherly Fischer[1] of Dresden. You will remember my telling you often of his wonderful faithfulness and devotion. An affection of the heart threatened him with death. When my wife entered his room he broke out, amid terrible sufferings: "Oh, Richard! Richard has forgotten me and thrown me aside." I had expected him last summer in Lucerne, but had not written to him again.

As soon as I heard of his condition I wrote to him, and now I receive the news of his death. My letter did not reach him in time for him to read it. These last days I have been writing an *envoi* to the memory of this dear friend. . . .

[1] Wilhelm Fischer, chorus master at the Dresden Opera. One of Wagner's earliest adherents.

"YOU WOULD THINK I STILL WAS IN THE 'RETREAT'"

At last I have my little lodging in order. If you were to enter you would think that I still was in the "Retreat." The same furniture, the accustomed writing table, the same green portières, engravings, everything—as you remember it. But the rooms are smaller and I have to divide them up. My miniature salon contains the Erard, the green sofa, with the two fauteuils which formerly were in the tea-room; hanging from the wall the Kaulbach, the Cornelius and the two Murillos; besides these a little cabinet with bookcase, work table and the well-known causeuse (of Lucerne memory). My bedroom I have had done in pale violet paper with a few green stripes to set it off. The Madonna della Sedia forms the only decoration. A very small room next to it contains the bath. This is the last time I shall furnish a place for myself.

As you know, I can hold to what I seriously decide upon. Well—never, never again will I settle anywhere. Heaven knows what this last attempt at settling down will end in. But

I know it will come to an end some time before
I die, and I know further that never again
will I arrange a nest for myself, but simply
await without any earthly possessions the
time when someone shall close my eyes.

AN OPINION OF GOUNOD

A few days ago I was invited to a musical
soirée, where sonatas, trios, etc., from
Beethoven's last period were played. I was
greatly provoked at the conception and interpretation of these, and am not to be caught
again soon. Still, I had a few experiences. I
sat next to Berlioz, who introduced me after
a while to his neighbour, the composer,
Gounod, an artist of agreeable appearance
and honest endeavour, but hardly of very
great talent. As soon as it became known
that I was present there was pressure from all
sides upon Berlioz to be introduced to me.
Curiously enough, they were all enthusiasts
about me, although they had studied my
scores without understanding German. I am
quite confused by all this. I am threatened
with several visits. I shall have to be on
my guard.

VICISSITUDES IN PARIS

"ENTIRELY BETWEEN OURSELVES"

Paris, November 29, 1859.

Nothing remains for me now but to make a final energetic effort and brush aside what has been an eternal obstacle in my path. However desolate and mismanaged my affairs may have been, I realise that much might become bearable and even acceptable if I could provide myself with the necessary material means so that at all times I could regulate my mode of life, my purposes, whatever I wish to undertake or to omit, according to my artistic requirements and judgment, without being eternally hampered by the lack of the one thing which in these days gives freedom and the possession of which makes it unnecessary for one to hesitate what to attempt or what to leave untouched. Lately I have realised this more strongly than ever —and yet I really always have felt it—that I can remain contemptuously indifferent to every failure, disappointment and lack of prospects, aye, to everything, everything of that kind; but that this plague to which I have referred revolts me and well-nigh drives me distracted.

187

To despise everything, to let nothing pollute the pure, inner source of my inspiraation, to be willing to dispense with recognition, even the possibility of having my works produced under my own direction, and then with gnashing teeth to strike my feet and wound them against this club which fate throws across my path in order to trip me up along the quiet, solitary way I am pursuing, that I cannot alter. I am and shall continue to be in a state of revolt against it, and, if I am to hold out at all,—being as I am and unable to change myself,—I must protest violently against such conditions, and stake everything on kicking this club out of my way once and for all. Fortunately I am in the humour just now to persuade myself that for a while at least it will be consonant with my disposition to devote myself to my material affairs. Doubtless you are not deceived by this; and if you opine that I would far prefer to seek the inward repose I long for in agreeable retirement among those in whom I can confide, with you, f. i., and devote myself to the creation of new works—remaining indifferent to their fate—let me tell you that you are quite right.

188

VICISSITUDES IN PARIS

(Which of course you understand, is entirely between ourselves!)

"COMPLETELY ESTRANGED FROM THE WORLD"

Paris, January 28, 1860.

No experience that I have had so far can be compared with what I observed and discovered at the first orchestral rehearsal for my concert, because it will have a determining influence upon my course for the rest of my life, and I shall be tyrannically governed by the consequences. I had my prelude to " Tristan " played for the first time; and—I realised, as if scales suddenly had fallen from my eyes, how completely I have become estranged from the world during the last eight years. This little prelude seemed so incomprehensibly new to the players that I was obliged to go over it note for note with my people as if I were guiding them to the discovery of precious stones in the shaft of a mine.

Bülow, who was present, confided to me that the performances of this piece which had been attempted in Germany had been accepted by the public simply on trust; but in itself it had remained wholly incomprehensible. I succeeded, however, in making the prelude understood both by the orchestra and the public—indeed, I am sure that it produced a profound impression. But do not question me how I brought it about. Enough that I now fully realise how impossible it is for me to think of creating further works until I have filled up the terrible chasm which yawns behind me. I must first produce my works under my own direction. And you know what that involves?

Child, that means that I must throw myself into a whirl of suffering and sacrifice in which the chances are that I will go under. Everything, yes, everything can be made possible, but only by having plenty of time and leisure for everything; by going step by step with singers and players; by never having to hurry, by never having to stop on account of lack of time, and by having all the proper means right at hand.

FIRST CONCERT—" UNENDING JUBILATION "

And now a few words about superficial occurrences. After the most unheard-of

190

labour, pains and torture I put through my first concert last Wednesday. The event was a festival. I cannot characterise it otherwise. I had already inspired the orchestra to the highest pitch of enthusiasm, and it hung on my eye and on my slightest beck and call.

It and the public received me with unending jubilation, and, " brilliant, astonishing, ravishing," was the verdict on each of my pieces on the programme. The whole affair created tremendous surprise. Wonderful experiences, conversions, feuilletonists (*Patrie*) all rushing up to me to kiss my hands. I was almost dead with exhaustion. That night was my last consecration of sorrow; but I must, I must go on.—It is my supreme duty.

The flower shall unfold itself to the world and perish; you shall keep the chaste bud.

Many kind greetings for Otto! Tell him that I love him! Farewell, dear, noble child! Live on gently and beneficently, and so strengthen me too!

A TRIBUTE FROM A " PLAIN CITIZEN "

Paris, March 3d, 1860.

First of all I will describe to you the object that stands on my mantel-piece in place of a clock. It is a wonderful affair. On a stand covered with red velvet rests a silver shield, the edge of which is covered with devices symbolic of my poems from " Rienzi " to " Tristan und Isolde." On the shield lies, in a silver wreath, one branch representing laurel, the other oak, a large leaf of silver sheet music, half rolled up and bearing in notation the principal motives from my operas.

A beautiful silver pen is placed across the music page, each end resting on a branch of the wreath. These branches are tied together with a gold ribbon, upon which is written:

"The heart of a right-minded man must overflow, before the sunny heights of great men. Dedicated to the great master with sincere admiration from Richard Weiland."

This Richard Weiland is a plain citizen of Dresden, whom I never met there, but who called on me one morning in Zurich—in the " Retreat "—and showed me the amusing critique of the Prague production of " Tannhäuser," with the simple statement that the overture, which under my own direction in

Dresden took only twelve minutes to play, had lasted twenty minutes there.—The gift, accompanied by a most modest letter I found here one evening on my return, tired out, after arranging for my choruses.—I now have the baton and this piece of silver plate.

PARIS ACQUAINTANCES

Through my concerts I have come in contact here with several deeply devoted and very intelligent people.

Gaspérini, a sensitive, highly intelligent and gifted physician, who, however, expects soon to give up his whole time to literary and poetic pursuits, a man of refined and handsome appearance and of profound sympathies, without, however, much original energy,—was mine even before I arrived, and is now the most ardent, persistent champion of my cause, for which he has found an opening in the *Courier du Dimanche*.

An admirable thinker and an unusually cultivated, unprejudiced, clear and refined intellect I have gained in Villot. This individual, who a short time ago married off a son, is curator of the Museum of the Louvre, a posi-

193

tion which places him in charge of all the works of art there. In a monumental work which cost him fifteen years of unintermittent industry, he has written a history of the Louvre collections. Now try to realise that this man—long before I knew him—owned all my scores, had studied them carefully, and is happy that through my mediation he has been able to procure from the Härtels a score of my " Tristan." He has greatly surprised me through the keenness of his judgment, especially, however, as regards the capacity of his own nation, to which he completely belongs as regards the manner in which he expresses himself, while intellectually he is far above it. He is of rare and refined intelligence. His offer to show me the treasures of the Louvre under his own guidance I have not yet availed myself of, and probably shall not be able to for a long, long time to come. Among others I may now mention to you the novelist Champfleury, whose pamphlet written on first impressions I have sent to you. He has thoughtful, friendly, yet wistful eyes. His intimate friend, the poet Baudelaire, has written me two wonderful letters, but does not wish to be introduced to me until he has

finished several poems which he intends dedi-
cating to me.

I have told you about Franck-Marie. He
has written some significant things about me;
but still is a stranger to me personally.

GUSTAVE DORÉ

Then there is a young artist, Gustave Doré,
who already enjoys a great reputation here.
He has made a drawing for *L'Illustration*,
in which he shows me conducting an orchestra
of spirits in an Alpine region. Then there
are many musicians and composers who have
declared themselves enthusiastically for my
cause, among them Gounod, a gentle, kind
man, and clearly gifted, although not highly
so; Louis Lacombe, Léon Kreutzer, Stephan
Heller.

Important as a deep thinking musician
is Sensale, who in future will play my
scores for me. A M. Perrin, well known as
a painter, also formerly director of the Opera
Comique and probably a future director of
the Grand Opera, is devoted to me and has
written beautifully about me in the *Revue
Européene*.

"BERLIOZ DEVOURED BY ENVY"

Berlioz is devoured by envy. My efforts
to keep him for my friend have come to
naught, because he cannot bear the brilliant
reception that has been accorded my music.
In truth, his own interests have been considerably prejudiced by my appearance in Paris
on the eve of the production of his "Trojans."
Moreover, his ill luck has given him a bad
wife, who allows herself to be bribed into
annoying her much suffering and weak husband. His attitude toward me has been a
constant wavering between friendly regard
and a rebound from one he envied. Very
tardy and yet so timed that he was not
obliged to refer to having heard my music
again, he published his critique, which you
probably have read. I felt myself justified
in answering his ambiguous, in fact malicious
reference to the "music of the future." You
will find this reply in the *Journal des Débats*
of February 22.

ROSSINI—THE "OLD EPICURE"

Rossini has behaved better. A joke about
my lack of melody had been attributed to him

196

and was eagerly spread by the German papers. Now he himself has 'dictated a denial, in which he declares that the only music of mine with which he is familiar is the " Tannhäuser " march, which pleased him greatly; moreover, that from all he knows about me he has great respect for me. This zeal on the part of the old epicure has surprised me.

Lastly let me announce another conquest, in the person of Marshal Magnan.[2] He attended all three concerts and manifested the deepest interest. As—unfortunately—it is important for me to have a man like him who moves in certain circles well posted about me, I called on him and really was surprised at his expressions of enthusiasm. He had been putting up a good fight for me and could not understand how anyone could hear in my music anything except just music, such as Gluck and Beethoven wrote, only with the characteristic stamp of genius " of a Wagner."

I cannot scare up any of my concert pro-

2 Barnard Pierre Magnan, b. 1791, d. 1865. Fought at Waterloo and figured prominently in the *coup d'état* of 1851.

grammes to-day, but you shall have one. You will observe that I have not made them too intimate. Your own doubts on that point decided me. Even the words to the " Tristan " selections contained only some explanation of the subject.

DETAILS OF THE CONCERTS

I will add a few words regarding the concerts. The string instruments were excellent; thirty-two violins, twelve violas, twelve violoncellos, eight double basses—an uncommonly sonorous body which you would have listened to with pleasure. But the rehearsals were insufficient and I could not secure the correct *piano* effect. The wind instruments were efficient only in part. All of them were wholly lacking in energy, and the oboe especially remained always pastoral in character and at no time struck a note of passion. The horns were wretched and cost me many a sigh.

The unhappy players excused themselves for their frequent wrong entrances, with the nervous effect which my manner of giving them their cues had upon them.

Trombones and trumpets were utterly without brilliance. All this was made good, however, by the really great enthusiasm which took possession of the whole orchestra from the first to the last player, and which manifested itself so continuously and so strikingly during the performances that Berlioz is said to have been considerably surprised by it.

"GENUINE FESTIVALS"

The three evenings developed into genuine festivals, and so far as evidences of enthusiasm are concerned the Zurich festivals were thrown completely into the shade. I held the attention of the audience from the outset. For the overture to "The Flying Dutchman" I have written a new close, which I like very much and which made a decided impression on the listeners also. Childish jubilation broke out immediately after the graceful melody in the " Tannhäuser " march, and on every recurrence of the melody the explosion was repeated. This spontaneous childishness really affected me agreeably, for I never have heard expressions of delight which manifested themselves so immediately. The first

199

time the Pilgrims' Chorus was sung it was hesitating and made no effect. Later it went better. The " Tannhäuser " overture, which was played with great virtuosity, always resulted in many recalls. The " Tristan " prelude was not played to my liking until the third concert. On that evening it gave me great delight. The public too seemed much affected by it, for when—the applause having subsided—an opponent ventured to hiss, there broke out a storm, so fierce, of such long duration, and always beginning over again, that poor me at my stand really became embarrassed, and I sought to indicate by gestures that I must ask them for Heaven's sake to stop, that I was fully satisfied; but that only seemed to add to their zeal, and the storm broke out anew. In short, I never have had such an experience.

All the selections from " Lohengrin " [3] made an uncommon impression from the very outset; orchestra and audience bore me, figuratively speaking, on their hands, and I cannot describe matters otherwise than by saying that—they were beautiful evenings.

[3] Prelude, introduction to Act III., and Bridal Chorus.

"WHY HANG MY HEAD SO SADLY?"

And now the child may well ask, with aston-ishment, why, instead of being satisfied with such exquisite experiences, I should hang my head so sadly?—Yes, that is a peculiar cir-cumstance, and all I can say is that festivals are easy!—and I do not need them. Such evenings remain something quite outside myself. They are dissipations, nothing more, and they leave the effect of every dissipation behind them; although, if I were differently constituted, it would be well enough. After all, perhaps I have accomplished much. I could rest in peace now, wait comfortably for what might turn up and for what I am as-sured must follow—glory, honour and Heaven knows what not. But what a fool I would be.

Imagine, even at the first concert I was *distrait* because a certain Receiver-General had not yet arrived from Marseilles. And what part was he to play?—He was the wealthy man who, according to Gaspérini's assur-ances, took a lively interest in my project for the performance of my operas in France, and who could easily be persuaded to aid me energetically in carrying it out.

I had thought of the possibility of a first performance of "Tristan" with German singers in Paris during May. That was the only goal toward which I was steering, and for which I was doing all this, and, above all, making insane efforts to put through these three concerts. My wealthy man was to come from Marseilles; the success of my music was to persuade him to declare himself ready to furnish the necessary guarantee for the operatic enterprise which I had in view. At last he arrives for the third concert, but has on this evening an engagement for a big dinner at Mirès, finds time, however, to visit the concert for an hour—is a superb Frenchman who expresses himself as greatly pleased, but later on considers that an attempt to give German opera here would be a doubtful enterprise, etc. And so that turned out to be another childish effort on my part!

And really I know all these things beforehand, and yet one hopes—and strives—because there is a goal, and a goal which it seems so necessary for me to reach. For, after all, I am here in this world, and my life has its meaning only in my ever having this goal in view and overlooking all else that lies between me and it. Only with it in view is my life worth while. How can I go on living if I turn my eyes from my goal and lower them to the chasm that parts me from it!

"ALL AGAIN IS NIGHT ABOUT ME"

Aye, indeed, others should do that for me, and keep me in the free air. But who has a right to demand that of anyone? Does not everyone live with some object in view, only that it does not always chance to be an eccentric object? And so it has happened, child, that the stupid master once more has been obliged in his solitude to look deep and long into that chasm.—Ah, what feelings come over him then. No landscape in Dante's "Inferno" has such frightful abysses!— Enough of this!—And the goal?—Still remains the only thing that gives me life! But how to reach it?

Aye, friend, so it goes! All again is night about me! If I no longer had any ambition it could so easily be otherwise. Now after unspeakable labour and torture I am obliged anew to work my way up out of the chasm, into which again I have plunged myself

almost purposely and blindly. As yet I can
not even see the height from which once more
I may allow my gaze to rest upon my goal.—
Recently when I saw the absolute necessity
of making every effort, to secure above all
a production of " Tristan," I said to myself,
" Now all is right. With such an ambition
there can be no more humiliation for you!
There can be nothing disgraceful in whatever
you do to secure the power and means to succeed, and to everyone who does not comprehend you as he sees you going an unaccus-
tomed way, you can cry out, ' What know
you of my goal? ' "—for he alone can comprehend me who comprehends this.

" WHAT AM I WITHOUT MY WORK? "

Every day brings new plans. This,
that and the other possibility is dangled
before my eyes. I am so insepara-
bly knit to this work, for which—and I
say this in all seriousness—I gladly would
offer my life as a sacrifice and willingly
swear not to live a day longer after I had
produced it. It may well follow from this that
I am now full of the idea that instead of

enduring all the labour and humiliation to
which I will be exposed in seeking the means
for " Parisian " successes, I should take upon
myself the torture, which seems easiest to
endure, and return to Dresden, be placed on
trial there, condemned and—so far as I am
concerned—pardoned, so that I will be able
without let or hindrance to look up the best
German theatre, wherever it may be, bring
out " Tristan " there and thus lift the sor-
cerous enchantment that now holds me in its
thrall. There is nothing else that seems to
me worth while. It appears to be about the
most sensible thing to do, and I reckon it an
unpardonable love of self for me to try to
avoid any suffering or humiliation that would
lead to the salvation of my work. For what
am I—without my work? Moreover, there is
another consideration! I have no faith in
my opera in France. Everything I do for
it here is undertaken against the inner voice,
which I can silence only through folly and
force. I have no faith in a French " Tannhäuser," nor in a French " Lohengrin," let
alone in a French " Tristan." Fortune re-
fuses to smile on whatever efforts I make in
this direction.

"WHAT DO I CARE FOR MY EARLIER WORKS?"

A daimon—my own, doubtless—is opposed to everything. Only through the command of a despot would it be possible to overcome all the obstacles which would be interposed between me and the stage of the Paris Opera. I have no real desire to overcome them. First of all, what do I care for my earlier works that have become almost indifferent to me? I surprise myself in an utter lack of interest in them. And then the French translations! I must regard them as absolutely impossible. The few stanzas that were translated for my concert caused me unspeakable trouble, and were execrable. In spite of everlasting efforts, not one act of my operas has been translated as yet, and what has been done on them disgusts me. The strange language doubtless is the chief reason that everything here remains essentially foreign to me. The torture of a conversation in French revolts me. Often I break off in the midst of an exclamation like one in despair, who says to himself, " After all, it is not possible, and all this is vain!" At such times I feel myself

206

wretchedly homeless. And if I ask myself, "Where do you belong, anyhow?" I can name no country, no city, no village.

"I LOOK LONGINGLY TOWARDS NIRVANA"

All is foreign, and often I look longingly toward the land of Nirvana, but Nirvana soon turns into "Tristan." You know the Buddhistic theory of creation; a breath clouds the crystalline clearness of the heavens, it swells, assumes shape, and at last the whole world stands before me in its impen-

etrable mass. Such will ever be my fate, as long as I have these unshriven spirits about me!

Something homelike I have with me in Bülow, but him, too, I soon will lose. The poor youth is working himself to death here, and I have seen little of him. He cannot visit me often, but it is agreeable to me to know that he is here. Heavens, it is such a

4 The Isolde motive.

pleasure to be able to speak naturally, and
he is the only one with whom I can do this.
He is, and continues, wholly devoted to me,
and often I am touched when I learn by the
merest chance of all the secret trouble he is
taking for me. He grows very sad when I
say to him that, in the end, all this will prove
useless, but before he goes I will give him
pleasure by telling him that you greet him
through me.

"I CANNOT DIE YET"

And now I must see that something is done
for me in the way of business, in an effort
to make up for the terrible devastation which
the expenses of my concerts have left in their
wake. It is proposed that I shall give the
same programme three times in Brussels
under conditions which assure me some slight
compensation. I suppose I will have to do
this. You may expect to hear from me from
there. London has also been suggested. 'Tis
sad, but then, you know, I cannot die yet.

And now, friend, it is just as well that I
close. Nothing very agreeable can come out
of this, and already I have allowed myself
to continue beyond all bounds. But at least

it helps to lift the weight from my heart that
I have been able to write to you again.
Thank you for this boon! Many fine greetings to Otto and the children. Let me know
how you all are! With faithful love.

"I GRIMLY SHOW MY TEETH"

Paris, April 10, 1860.

You naughty child! Your last letter, too
—and that was long ago—told me so little,
hardly anything about yourself. Is my own
silly fate always to be considered the only
thing worth talking about! I am quite in
doubt as to whether these lines will find you
still in Rome. It would be just like you to
leave there without saying a word about it
to me, or letting me know when and whither
you go! You see I am scolding; a few days
ago I would have been more gentle about it,
but now, day by day, it annoys me more and
more. Please write me at length how you are.
About all the things you are seeing. Your
daily life. The acquaintances you are making, and the state of your health, and everything of that sort.

You promised that now and then I might
have a look into your stereopticon. Have I

suddenly been wholly excommunicated? Oh! one can tell where you are!

For once I really ought not to talk about myself at all, but what do I know about you! Nothing, except that I know nothing. Truly philosophical knowledge this! And about myself? Dearest child, no one will ever be able to make anything in reason out of me. Above all, no one with any intelligence. For instance: Just now I am being congratulated by all intelligent people, and everyone thinks I must be soaring among heights of bliss and delight because I have obtained the incredible promise that one of my operas is to be performed in Paris. " Can he ask anything more?" they say. And now picture this to yourself—never have I found the whole thing more tiresome than just now, and to everyone who congratulates me I grimly show my teeth. I happen to be built that way!

FRENCH MUSICAL TASTE

Whoever stands by quietly and watches the life of a nation as gifted, and also as incredibly light-hearted as France, and is able to interest himself in everything that may serve

MATHILDE WESENDONK
1860
From a photograph taken in Rome

for its development and progress, cannot be blamed if he sees in the manner in which a French " Tannhäuser " may be received, a critical test of the capacity of this people for artistic advancement.

Consider the wretched state of French art at this moment; that poetry is something wholly foreign to this nation, and that in its place it substitutes rhetoric and sonorous phrases. With the French language completely centred upon itself, and its resulting incapacity to take over the poetic element which it lacks from another language, the only method which remains is to have poetry influence the French through music. The truth is, however, that the French lack originality in music, and that all their music has come from elsewhere. From the outset French musical taste has been formed by the contact of Italian and German music, and really is nothing more than a meeting point of these two schools.

Gluck, critically considered, only taught the French how to bring music into harmony with the rhetorical style of French tragedy. With real poetry we are not concerned in his case at all. That is the reason why, since then, the Italians have occupied the field almost exclusively, for it always was a matter of rhetorical method of expression, rather than of music itself, let alone poetry. What utterly hopeless conditions have resulted, and still result from this, is incredible. Lately, in order to gauge the singers at the Opera, I was obliged to listen to a new work by a Prince Poniatowski.[5] What an experience! What a longing came over me for the plainest Swiss mountain valley! I felt as if I had been assassinated when I reached home, and all hope of accomplishing anything had vanished. Since then, however, I have learned how opposing influences may gather strength and impetus from such horrible conditions.

"YOUR WORK REJECTED, WE ABANDON HOPE"

"You see," people say to me, "how matters stand and what we expect and demand of you!" This is said to me by people who have not attended the Opera for twenty years,

5 Probably "Pierre de Medicis." After Sedan, Josef Poniatowski, Prince of Monte Rotondo, followed Napoleon III. into exile and died at Chiselhurst, Eng., in 1873.

and who have confined themselves to attending the concerts and quartettes at the Con-
servatoire, and finally—without any personal
acquaintance with me—made a study of my
scores. They include not only musicians, but
painters, scientific men, and even—states-
men. They say to me, " Nothing in the least
like what you are bringing to us ever has
been offered to this public, for with music
you bring us poetry in its highest form. You
bring it complete, and wholly in your own
way, and independent of every influence
such as has been exerted by our institutions
upon the creative artists who desired to produce something for us. You bring it entire,
and with the greatest power of expression.
Even the most ignorant Frenchman would
not desire to change anything in your work.
He will be obliged to accept it or reject it,
just as it is, and herein lies the vast importance which we attach to the impending
event. Your work rejected, we will know
where we stand, and abandon all hope; accepted, and that at once (for the Frenchman
cannot be influenced in any other way), all of
us will breathe freely again. For neither
science nor literature, but theatrical art

alone, with its instantaneous and universal effect, can exert a strong influence upon the genius of our nation, and change its point of view. Finally—we have confidence in the greatest and most lasting success for your undertaking! "

It is a fact that even the director of the Opera, now that he has become thoroughly acquainted with the subject, goes about telling everyone that in " Tannhäuser " he at last can count upon a real " succès d'argent."

"THE SUREST GUARANTEE IS MY POVERTY "

Meanwhile, in Brussels, I have had considerable intercourse with a remarkable man, an aged, knowing, clever and uncommonly experienced diplomat,[6] who strongly advises me not to underrate the French. He argues that, whatever people may think or say, it yet remains an incontestable fact that at the present time the French are the real prototypes of European civilisation, and that to make a deep impression upon them means to have made a deep impression upon all Europe.

6 State Councillor Klindworth, a relic of the Metternich period.

All this sounds very encouraging, and I see that I cannot rid myself of the important role I am to play in the world. Curiously enough, however, I do not seem to care a rap either for Europe or for the world, and at the bottom of my heart I keep saying to myself, " How does all this concern you? " But I realise, as I have just said, that I cannot break away from it; my daimon will take care of that. The surest guarantee that I am bound to influence Europe is—my poverty!

I make this confession to you in order that you may not reach any wrong conclusions about me, and above all that you have no fear lest this conceited assumption about myself lead me to something rash, something that really lies beyond me. These Paris concerts have placed me in a difficult position. I undertook Brussels only to help myself in my plight, but with just the opposite result, so that when I left there I said to myself, " Si jamais on me prend à faire de l'argent (just as Rossini once said, after the failure of an opera on the score of which he had worked very carefully, " Si jamais on me prend à soigner ma partition ").

GERMANY REMAINS SILENT

The German attitude toward me is one of complete silence, and if ever I am to meet my Tristans and my Nibelungs in this life, I shall be obliged to perform a miracle, and walk the waves of this holy existence. Therefore, I accept the hopes of my Parisian friends, and especially of my Opera director. But at present, as everything that is glorious unfortunately keeps one waiting for its consummation, I am not at all indisposed to sell myself to a Russian general, who soon is expected here, in order to persuade me to undertake a " Tannhäuser " expedition to St. Petersburg. Join with me in laughing over this, I beg of you. It is the only way one can help me with these ridiculous burdens, which a world in need of salvation loads upon the back of its expected Saviour!

Yesterday they sent me from Brussels my photographic likeness. It seems to have turned out very well. At once I thought of you. If you will soon send me a pretty letter and tell me when you are returning to Zurich, I will send a copy to Mr. Stunzig, or to anyone else whom you designate, so as to let you know what I look like nowadays; and it should be hung in the gallery over the piano.

As you have taken all your personal belongings with you to Rome, there will be no friend to greet you on your return unless I am there, even if only in the gallery.

THE ARTIST A PLAYTHING

Paris, May 2, 1860.

And the artist?—Poor fellow! He is the plaything of his own inner consciousness, and yet he is so ridiculously constituted that he can stand out against this eternal opposition. Yes, always to be in opposition, never to find complete inward repose, always driven, lured, and then rejected, that really is the ever-seeming process of his life. It makes his inspiration bloom like a flower of despair—I know that from experience, and I know you feel this in sympathy with me! But who would be other than he is?

A HIT AT LISZT'S PRINCESS

Paris, May 23, 1860.

Liszt has become wholly unreliable, so far as keeping a secret is concerned, and this, not from inward conviction, but because through his manifestly abused good-nature, he has been brought to an unlovely state of dependence. But I have let him—or, rather, unfortunately both of them—know decidedly that I no longer can correspond with him (or them).[7] The poor fellow silently sacrifices everything, and suffers, and believes this cannot be changed, yet he continues to love me, and always will remain to me a noble and very dear man. You can imagine then how touchingly a greeting occasionally finds its way to us. We discover the means now and then to press each other's hand in confidence, like a loving couple that has been parted by the world. Thus yesterday, there arrived by telegraph the warmest congratulations upon my birthday. I smile inwardly over such occurrences and am rejoiced.

HOW TO POSE FOR A PHOTOGRAPH

You will receive my portrait just as soon as I know when I can address it to Zurich. It

[7] This is a hit at Liszt's *amie,* the Princess Carolyne Sayn-Wittgenstein, and explains the practical cessation of the Wagner-Liszt correspondence.

is the best I have had taken. This seems especially remarkable to me, because it has turned out so well in spite of most unfavourable circumstances, and especially because such a quiet, unaffected expression has been secured. I was greatly put out, and genuinely plagued by the Brussels musicians, to leave a photograph behind me as a souvenir. It was raining (Otto knows it always rains in Brussels), and I had not intended to go to the studio. Finally, late in the day they fetched me. I had no umbrella, was obliged to conduct that evening, had to climb up five flights of stairs, and I expressed to the artist my indignation that he should attempt to achieve anything tolerable under such circumstances. The confidence with which the artist (an excellent one, to be sure) met my objections put me into good humour, and with the declaration, " It really will be remarkable if it turns out well," I took up my position in astonishment at the whole proceeding, simply thinking to myself, " Well, for the Brussels folk the result may be good enough! " Now, however, I can remember that I became conscious with what incredible swiftness the brain is guided by certain moods, and leaps from

things at hand to circumstances quite re-
mote.

Shortly before this I had been photographed
in Paris, and the barbarian who called himself
an artist had thought it well, before I myself had become aware of it, to place me in a
most affected pose, with eyes turned side-
ways. I am disgusted with the portrait which
resulted, and have declared that it makes me
look like a sentimental Marat. This unfortunate counterfeit was used for *L'Illustration* and—with further distortion—is making the rounds of all the illustrated papers
(at the present time in England). My disgust with it unconsciously persuaded me at
the Brussels sitting to seek an entirely different and more decent expression, so that I
would present a natural, calm, and intelligent
appearance. The irony of the whole proceeding put me, quick as a flash, into the right
mood. Everything seemed to vanish, and I
looked calmly out upon the world, as if it did
not concern me at all. Possibly I may have
entertained the wish to look at Jupiter. Perhaps it will seem to you as if Jupiter really
had shone for me for a few moments.

VICISSITUDES IN PARIS

" ' TRISTAN ' REMAINS A MIRACLE!"

Paris, early August, 1860.

What a poet I am! Heaven help me for
making such a claim.—This wretched translation of " Tannhäuser " has made me so conceited. Just now, when it is necessary to go
over it word for word, I appreciate for the
first time how compact and incapable of being
changed the poem is. A word or phrase
dropped, and both my translator and myself are obliged to confess that something
which cannot be spared has been sacrificed.
At the beginning I believed that a few slight
changes might be made, but we were obliged
to give up all of them as impossible. I was
quite astonished, and found when I compared
myself with others, that there are very few
whom I could credit with an equal gift. In
short, I have been obliged to acknowledge to
myself that the poem could not have turned
out better. What do you say to this? I
could more easily improve the score. Here
and there, for instance, are passages for the
orchestra that might be more expressive and
richer.

" Tristan " is, and remains a miracle! How

I ever created such a work becomes more and
more incomprehensible. In reading it over
again I open eyes and ears wide! How frightfully I will have to expiate this work if I try
to have it performed. I clearly anticipate
the most unheard-of suffering from it, for I
do not attempt to conceal from myself that
in the demands it will make upon the performers, it goes far beyond anything that
now is even dreamed of as possible. Remark-
ably sympathetic artists who are entirely
equal to such a task are born but rarely into
this world, and yet, even while listening only
to the orchestra, I cannot resist the temptation of trying to have it produced.

"PARSIFAL" OUTLINED

"Parzival" again has been awakening
within me. I see the subject more clearly
before me. If once it ripens to fruition, the
execution of this poem will become an unspeakable joy for me. But many years may
pass before that consummation! This time,
too, I should like to have the poem stand by
itself. I shall hold off as long as I can, and
occupy myself with it only when it takes com-

plete possession of me! Then the wonderful process of creation will enable me to forget all my misery.

Shall I gossip a little about it? Did I ever tell you that the fabulously wild messenger of the Grail is to be one and the same being with the seductive woman of the second act? Since I have had that inspiration, everything connected with the subject has become clear to me. This wonderfully terrible creature, who serves the Knights of the Grail with the tireless zeal of a slave, executes the most unheard-of commissions, lies in a corner, awaiting only the command to carry out something uncommonly laborious—at times disappears utterly, no one knows how or whither.

Then suddenly she reappears, but fearfully exhausted, wretched, pale, and gruesome, yet just as tireless as before, and serving the Holy Grail like a dog, although her attitude towards the Knights seems to be one of secret contempt. Her eyes seem ever to roll restlessly in search of the right one.—She has been deluded more than once—has not found him. She herself does not know just what she is looking for, she is guided only by instinct.

When Parzival, the Fool, arrives in this domain, she cannot take her eyes off him. Wonderful things must be transpiring within her; what, she knows not herself, but she remains near him. She is repellent to him—and yet she attracts him, but he comprehends nothing. (This means—work for the poet! Only the way the thing is done can make it plain!) But let me try to explain it to you, and listen to me as Brünnhilde listened to Wotan.—This woman is in a constant state of restlessness and excitement. The old esquire often has observed this on former occasions, shortly before her disappearances. This time she seems under a terrible strain. What is passing through her mind? Is she dreading another flight? Does she desire to be spared it? Has she hope—to be able to end everything? With what hope has Parzival inspired her? Manifestly she is directing a silent appeal to him.—But everything remains dark and obscure. No clear perception, only impulse and mental dusk. Crouched in a corner, she watches the painful scene of Anfortas. She bestows a wonderfully searching (sphinx-like) gaze on Parzival, but he, too—is stupid, comprehends nothing, only wonders—remains silent. He is ejected. The messenger of the Grail collapses with a shriek. A moment later she vanishes. (Again she is obliged to wander.)

Now can you guess who is the wonderfully enchanting woman whom Parzival finds in the strange palace to which his knightly love of adventure leads him? Imagine what happens there, and how everything turns out. But for the present I will enlighten you no farther!

Paris, August 10, 1860.

Meanwhile, Queen Victoria has taken it into her head that she would like to hear " Lohengrin " this winter. The manager of Covent Garden has looked me up. He says the Queen would like to have " Lohengrin " given in English—some time in February. As yet I know nothing about particulars. How comical it would be if I were to hear this work for the first time given in English.

" I AM LIKE ONE DEAD "

Paris, November 17, 1860.

Another bulletin, my child! I am improving—but slowly and tediously. The weather

225

does not favour me at all, but keeps putting me back all the time. Nevertheless, I have attended to a little piece of business, the first since I have been convalescing. I have been to the bookbinder. The piano score of "Tristan" has at last been published. I have ordered the Härtels to send several copies to Zurich direct; also one for Mme. Wille, but for my friend I want something special. I have had a copy sent to me here. I am going to have it bound according to my own taste, and I shall transmit it to you myself. Unfortunately the copy arrived here at the worst period of my illness. You can imagine my distress. I was obliged to see it lying there without being able to do anything about it. Now at last I have been to the bindery. Whether the thing turns out as I would like it, I must, I am sorry to say, doubt. People here are so lacking in imagination and originality.

Probably I shall have to put up with something wholly commonplace, and you must make allowances for my good intentions. Some time may elapse before it is finished, and you will be obliged to accept it as a birthday and Christmas gift in one.

As regards things in general, I am like one—
dead! I hardly can describe my state of
mind differently! I keep perfectly quiet, like
one who has lost all interest in life. Future
performances of my latter works, nothing but
mist and dreams. No zeal, no desire!

" FAME NO LONGER ATTRACTS ME "

For the 23d of December.

I chance to find just now a sheet of paper
of my colour, and on it I send you, my friend,
my birthday congratulations.

What shall I wish for you, what offer to
you? A life of endless trouble and restlessness persuades me that the thing most to be
desired is—perfect peace! I myself have
such a deep longing for it that I invoke it for
others, and especially for her who is everything to me, as the greatest of all gifts. It
is something so difficult to attain. One who
is not born with it rarely achieves it, and only
a total conquest of self will yield it to him as
the prize of victory. Whoever adjusts his
life thus, and so shapes his character in relation to this life, he will be able, on the whole,
to view it in perfect calmness; although the

trifles that keep coming up from day to day will excite his spleen, and make him impatient and restless.

In what a strange condition I am! Everything, almost without exception, which sets the world in motion leaves me cold and untouched. Fame no longer attracts me; success only so far as it may keep me from want. To undertake anything serious from either cause never would be possible for me. Whether I am in the right or not is a matter of indifference to me, since I know from experience how incredibly small is the number of those who are so constituted as even to understand another.

My most natural and pardonable desire to bring about a fully commensurate performance of my various works has cooled off considerably, and especially during this last year. Meddling with musicians, singers, etc., again, has caused me many a sigh, and strengthened my feeling of resignation in this direction.

I am forced to realise more and more how completely my art creations have estranged me from the rigid art conditions of these modern times. I am free to acknowledge that

now—if I suddenly look at my " Nibelung "
or " Tristan "—I awake with a start as if
out of a dream and say to myself, " Where
have you been?—You have been dreaming!
Open your eyes and acknowledge that you are
face to face with reality! "

Yes, I no longer will deny the fact that I
consider my last works absolutely impossible
of performance. If the impulse still lingers
within me to bring about their performance,
this again becomes possible only by allowing
my mind to wander through the realms of
dreams.

" WHERE SHALL I FIND CONSOLATION? "

Oh! my child! where shall I find my sole,
sole consolation?—Once, indeed, I discovered
the heart and the soul which, in moments like
these, wholly understood me, and to whom I
was dear because it was her privilege to understand and comprehend me so completely! See,
then, to this soul I fly; like one completely
exhausted my limbs give way under me, and I
allow myself to sink into the delicate ether
of her friendly spirit. All my experiences,
my unheard-of emotional distress, cares and

sorrows, are like refreshing dew distilled from a storm-flower to cool my burning temples. In it I find refreshment and finally a sense of repose, sweet repose. I am loved—understood!

And this peace I bring to you! May you find in the sweet consciousness of what you are to me—my angel of peace, the guardian of my life—the noble spring which purls over all that is arid in your existence! Share this feeling of peace with me, and receive it from me to-day in the fulness of the blessing it confers upon me as I lose myself wholly in you!

"TRISTAN" WITH VIARDOT-GARCIA

Paris, February 12, 1861.

Among those in so-called high society, there is a lady with whom I formerly had a slight acquaintance, and who has attracted my attention to a greater degree than formerly. She is the Countess Kalergis, the niece of the Russian Minister of State Nesselrode, whom I have told you of before. Last summer she spent some time in Paris, looked me up and persuaded me to have Klindworth come from

London in order to have some music with her. I sang the second act of " Tristan " with Viardot-Garcia; quite among ourselves, only Berlioz was present. We also had some things out of the " Nibelung," for the first time since I have been away from you. My attention was drawn to this lady by observing her peculiar weariness, contempt for the world, and disdain, which might have remained a matter of indifference to me if I had not observed in addition her manifestly deep longing for music and poetry, which, under these circumstances, seemed to me somewhat significant.

However great her talent in this respect, she herself became an object of interest to me since she was the first person I had met who surprised me by a most spontaneous and really grand comprehension of my unfortunate situation.

Shall I conceal from you that everything gives way to the one thought of being able to see you again, if only for an hour? No, my child, I will not conceal this from you. And even if you came at the risk of not seeing me as I really am, and as I would be when with you, yet I—egotist that I am—would

bless the hour during which it would be
vouchsafed me to gaze into your eyes once
more.

"I AM TIRED OF BEING NOTHING BUT A NUISANCE"

Paris, April 6, 1861.

Really I am growing tired of always being
nothing but a nuisance to my friends. This
bitter feeling is all that remains to me of the
Paris adventure. The mischance itself has
left me quite indifferent. If I had looked
only to a material success I might have gone
about many things differently; but that is—
the very thing I do not care for. The only
kind of material success I could wish for is
that which results from an artistic one. The
possibility of securing a really fine performance of one of my works nerved me to the
effort. But when I realised the impossibility
of this, I was through with the whole thing
and defeated in advance. What then happened to me was nothing more than just
punishment for indulging in another illusion.
I cannot say that it touched me deeply. My
work as it was performed seemed to me something quite so unfamiliar that what happened

to it did not concern me at all and I regarded
the whole affair simply as a great hubbub. If
the occurrence have consequences or not leaves
me cold. The only feeling I have in regard
to it is—weariness, disgust.

My child, whither have flown the happy Calderon evenings? What sinister planet has
robbed me of the "Retreat" I had earned?
Believe me, whatever others may say,—from
the moment I left the "Retreat" my star
was doomed to wane. All that is left to it
now is to fall.

My best regards to Otto. His presence here
in these bad times was more of a grief than
a joy to me, although I must give you my
word that his sympathy and interest, indeed
his whole attitude, touched me deeply. But
I could be so little to him personally. There
was constant hurry, and the final failure of
my enterprise became a certainty just at the
time he was here. During the rehearsals,
when my own work became more strange and
unrecognisable to me, I suffered most.

The performances, on the other hand, had the
effect of physical blows that awakened me
from my inward suffering to a consciousness
of sad reality.

WAGNER AND HIS ISOLDE

HEARS "LOHENGRIN" FOR THE FIRST TIME

Vienna, May 11, 1861.

I have just been attending a rehearsal of
"Lohengrin." I cannot keep to myself the
incredibly deep impression of this first hearing of my work under such beautiful and
sympathetic conditions, both from an artistic
and a human point of view. I lived twelve
years of my life over again!—such years!
You were right in so often wishing that this
joy might be mine! But nowhere else could
I have found it so completely as here. Ah!
if you could only be here to-morrow!

A thousand tender greetings!

RETURNS TO PARIS

Paris, June 15, 1861.

Ah! my child! if I did not have you, things
would go badly with me. Hold to that, and
consider that, in saying this to you, I have
said everything! But really I no longer can
say that I live! Some time, perhaps, I shall
again take pleasure in something—if ever I
get away from here; that would be the first
step!

234

DEATH OF ANOTHER PET

Paris, Prussian Legation,
July 12, 1861.

As for myself, I never expect to settle down again anywhere. This conclusion I have reached after my last sad and infinitely wearying experience. It is not ordained for me ever to woo my muse in the lap of cheerful domesticity. From within and without every attempt to gratify this desire, which is such a strong trait of my nature, comes to nought with ever-growing certainty, and is thrown all into a heap by my daimon, whenever it beckons me alluringly. It is not for me, and the quest for rest always becomes in my case a cause of pain and sorrow. And so I consecrate the rest of my life to wandering. Perhaps now and then it will be vouchsafed me to rest and refresh myself awhile in the shade of some quiet spring.

This is the only blessing that still seems reserved for me.

Finally the little dog which you sent me, from your own sick-bed, died, suddenly and strangely. It seems as if he must have been run over on the street, and have received some internal injury. After five hours, during

235

which the sweet, friendly creature lay before me without so much as a plaint, but growing weaker all the time, he silently breathed his last. Not a rod of earth belonged to me in which I might bury this dear little friend. Partly by diplomacy, partly by force, I secured a spot in Sturmer's little garden, where I myself secretly interred my poor dead pet under a bush.

With this dear little dog I buried much!— now I will wander, and in my wanderings I no longer will have a little companion.

THE MUSICAL LION OF WEIMAR

Vienna, August 19, 1861.

Of course, rest and enjoyment were out of the question in Weimar. From near and far everybody seemed to throng about me, in order to see me again, or just to see me. Really, I was obliged every half hour to relate the story of my life to this or that person. At last despair yielded to my old mad humour, and everyone here was greatly elated by my sportiveness. I could not allow myself to be serious. In fact, I no longer can, without running the risk of being completely overcome by my feelings. This is a temperamental failing of mine which is gaining the upper hand more and more. I guard against it as best I can, for it seems to me sometimes as if I simply must flood away in tears.

And so I took a friendly farewell of Weimar. Above all I have borne away with me a delightful souvenir of Liszt, who now intends to leave Weimar, where he was unable to plant anything, and, so far as the near future is concerned, go into the unknown. His "Faust" really gave me great pleasure, and the second part (Gretchen) made a deep and unforgettable impression upon me. I was greatly grieved that it was impossible to have the work produced except in a most mediocre manner. Everything had to be ready with one rehearsal. Hans, who conducted, performed a miracle in his endeavour to have the performance at least tolerable.

And so this was the goal of all the sacrifices made by " lucky " Liszt—that he could not even wring from this wretched world the most ordinary means to a good performance of his work! How this experience strengthened me in my own spirit of resignation!

WAGNER AND HIS ISOLDE

A PORTRAIT OF MATHILDE

Vienna, September 28, 1861.

Oh! noble, splendid child! To-day I really
should add nothing more to this exclamation.
All else that I can say seems null! Music
has converted me into an explosive creature,
and the exclamation point is really the only
punctuation mark that suffices for me whenever I turn over my music! But, after all, that
is the old enthusiasm, without which I could
not exist. For suffering, sorrow, even anger
and ill-humour, take this enthusiastic turn
with me—which probably is the reason why
I am such a bother to others.

How much one can accomplish in Zurich!
One might rummage through Vienna, Paris
and London without finding anything as successful in the photographic line as this production of Herr Keller's. Child, how beautiful you are! Words cannot express it!—
Heavens! In such a heart everything must be
regally up-borne. The most wretched beggar
whom it admits into its communion must soon
feel his head touching the clouds!—Then, too,
the birth-pangs of exalted regeneration are
stamped upon these features which once wore

so child-like a smile!—Aye! God now dwells
in the child!—Bow your heads!

"DREAMS" AGAIN

Then, too, I got out the large green
portfolio for the first time. I had kept
it locked since my departure from Lucerne. Now I produced the key in order
to have another look at its treasures. Heavens, how they affected me! Two photographs,
the birth place of " Tristan "—the Green Hill
with the " Retreat," and the Venetian palace.
Then, too, the birth certificates with the first
sketches, wonderful germs; also the verses of
dedication with which I sent the pencilled
sketches of the first act to the child. What
joy these verses gave me! They are so pure,
so genuine!—I also found the pencilled leaf
of the song from which I developed the night
scene. Heaven knows this song pleased me
more than the proud scene itself. Heavens,
it is more beautiful than all else that I have
created. I tremble to the very depths of my
being when I listen to it! And how can I
allow these memories to conjure up the past
in my heart without a feeling of infinite bliss!

How should this be possible?—I closed the
portfolio again. But the last letter with the
picture I opened once more, and cried out,
"Pardon! Pardon!—I will not invoke you
again!"

"THE GRAY HORIZON OF THE FUTURE"

Paris, December 21, 1861.

I had to break out into loud laughter as I
looked up from my work and saw the Tuile-
ries and the Louvre opposite! For know that
I am now rummaging about in Nuremberg,
and in company with square, solid people.
My only resource was to mingle with such
folk. The return journey from Venice to
Vienna was very tedious. Two long nights
and a day I sat helplessly hemmed in between the past and the present, and travelling toward the gray horizon of the future.
I must work on something new—or—there
will be an end to everything. Unfortunately
my visual horizon is contracting. Nothing
suffices to claim my attention, and anything
of local interest, or connected therewith, even
the greatest pictures in the world, cannot
draw me out of myself or interest me. I can

merely differentiate between day and night, light and darkness. Really it is a kind of death outwardly, and toward everything without; I see only inward pictures, and they demand to be expressed in music.

ENTER THE "MEISTERSINGER"

But no pictures of passion could I conjure up within me during that gray journey. The world seemed to me like a toy. That reminded me of Nuremberg, where I spent a day last summer, and where much that is pretty is to be seen.

It echoed in my memory like an overture to the "Mastersingers of Nuremberg." After reaching my hotel in Vienna, I worked out the plan with extraordinary rapidity, and it was a pleasure for me to realise while doing so that my memory was absolutely clear, and how readily my imagination worked hand in hand with my inspiration. It was my salvation, the kind of salvation that incipient insanity sometimes affords. I immediately put all my other affairs in order, shot a year-long bolt in front of "Tristan," and declined with thanks invitations to triumphs in several cities of my glorious German Fatherland; then came here in order " to forget that I am alive."

And now be tolerant of my Nuremberg mastersingers! They will turn out very decent fellows, and probably as early as the beginning of next winter will make their appearance on the German stage, after which I shall pay little heed to them.

" TRISTAN " I OWE TO YOU

To produce " Tristan " continues the main object of my ambition. That once accomplished, I shall have little more to do in this world, and shall gladly go to rest with master Cervantes. That I should have composed " Tristan " I owe to you, and I thank you from the depths of my heart in all eternity.

SUCH STUFF AS DREAMS ARE MADE OF

VI

Like so many of his hopes, Wagner's dream of "Tristan" in Vienna came to nought. The "Meistersinger" project was, however, taking shape. He arranged with the Schotts of Mayence to publish it, and in order to be conveniently near them he settled in February, 1862, in Biebrich, on the opposite bank of the Rhine. From Paris he had sent the manuscript of the completed drama to Mathilde. In a letter from Biebrich, March 12, 1862, he calls her attention to the fact that this is the first time she has been obliged to become acquainted with a poem of his through her own reading, instead of having it read to her by himself.

On one occasion, when the Schotts appear to have refused him a further pecuniary advance until more of the manuscript of the score had been turned in, he indirectly invoked Mathilde's aid. Bethinking himself of her poems which he had set to music, he went over them with a Mayence singer; then a party consisting of himself, the vocalist (Fraülein Genast), the Bülows, who were visiting him, and his friend, Wendelin Weissheimer, a conductor at the Mayence Opera, drove across the Rhine bridge at Castel and through Mayence to the Schotts' villa at Laubenheim. There, with Bülow " at the piano," Fräulein Genast sang the five songs, " Dreams " included, for the benefit of the head of the house of Schott, who is represented by Weissheimer as gleefully rubbing his hands as he walked up and down the room while listening to the music, and finally taking the manuscript from Wagner and carefully locking it in a closet.

The remaining letters are interesting, for everything Wagner wrote is characteristic. But it was already noticeable in the Paris letters that, while these teemed with graphic descriptions of people and events, they were not, on the whole, as introspective or as deeply steeped in the psychological romance of which Mathilde was the heroine and he the hero as his journals and letters from Venice. The letters become fewer, and there is even less of this fascinating introspective quality in the correspondence which follows the Paris

MATHILDE WESENDONK
(1864)
After a Bas Relief by Joseph Kopf

period. Wagner was at work again, and on a thoroughly sane topic, the " Meistersinger "; since leaving the Green Hill he had seen Mathilde but rarely, and—Cosima had appeared upon the scene. Wendelin Weissheimer says significantly, with reference to certain episodes of the Bülows' Biebrich visit to Wagner, " coming events cast their shadows before." In fact, the heart, the soul, of the correspondence lie in the passages I already have given.

"ONE LOVES BUT ONCE"

Once more indeed the old love flared up in clear flame. It was at Penzing, near Vienna, in June, 1863. Harassed by debts, Wagner seems to have sought relief from his misery by writing to Frau Wille, pleading that he could not write to Mathilde for fear his surcharged heart would lead him to say too much.

" Again," he writes, " I have been looking through the green portfolio which she sent me when I was in Venice. How much suffering I have experienced since then! And now once more the old enchantment hovers about me! Sketches for 'Tristan', for the music to her poems! Ah! dearest! one loves but once, and however intoxicating and alluring whatever may come to us thereafter, I now well know that I never shall cease to love her alone. You will understand how to honour the innocence of this assurance, and to pardon the frankness of my confession."

THE VILLA CLOSED TO HIM

Frau Wille, being a novelist, knew her cue, and she must have sent this letter to Mathilde just as she had done with the one which Wagner wrote her from Venice five years before. Otherwise neither of these epistles would have been found in this correspondence. Nevertheless, when, in April, 1864, the composer's creditors in Penzing threatened him with arrest, and he let drop a hint that he would like to find refuge from them on the Green Hill, this was not found "convenient." While Wesendonk had allowed Wagner to correspond with his wife, the meetings between Wagner the composer and Mathilde had been few, and Otto doubtless did not care to start up the gossips of Zurich again by having him

in his villa or even in the " Retreat " for any
considerable length of time. In consequence
he applied for refuge to Frau Wille, who
received him and cared for his comfort as
gladly and as tenderly as if she had been the
Isolde instead of only the Brangäne of
the Zurich romance. She had her reward,
for her reminiscences of this visit are among
the most interesting things that have been
published about Wagner. Moreover, when,
after about a month's stay at Marienfeld, he
went to Stuttgart, where the emissary of
King Louis found him, it was to her he wrote
announcing the wonderful change which thus
had been wrought in his fortunes.

KIND REGARDS FROM COSIMA

Minna Wagner died in Dresden in 1866.
Cosima secured a divorce from Von Bülow in
1869 and married Wagner the following
year. His first visits with her were to Frau
Wille and to the Wesendonks. The composer's last letter to Mathilde was written
July 28, 1871, from Tribschen near Lucerne,
and in the last sentence he sends her greetings from his wife. " Kind regards from

Cosima " would be a prosaic ending for the story of Wagner and his Isolde, but, fortunately, something still remains to be said.

MATHILDE HIS GREATEST INSPIRATION

Mathilde was the inspiration of all the great works which Wagner created after " Lohengrin." " Rheingold," " Walküre," " Siegfried," " Götterdämmerung," " Tristan und Isolde," " Meistersinger," even " Parsifal," to all these, in one way or another, she stood in intimate relationship. The first inspiration for the " Rheingold " score came to him on that tour in search of health which he made with money furnished by Otto, doubtless on Mathilde's urging. Note by note she watched the " Nibelung " scores develop, until, again inspired by her, Wagner turned from "Siegfried " to " Tristan." Needless to repeat here that she was his Isolde. It can be read in line after line of the foregoing letters and journals. " Meistersinger? " Was it not she who recalled the subject to his mind? " Parsifal? " He outlined it for her when it first began to take shape in his mind as " Parzival! " " Götterdämmerung? " It was not

completed until years after Wagner's flight
from Zurich; yet what is it but a continua-
tion of the scores which Mathilde's " dusk
man " played for her in the music-room of the
villa on the Green Hill? She even knew
something of his plans for " The Victors,"
which he did not live to carry out. Even
when Wagner reached back into the past and
rewrote the Venusberg scene in " Tannhäuser," he was not content but that his plan
and the reasons for it must be communicated
to her in detail, in order that she might have
a share in that work too! Mathilde Wesendonk was not a genius. But she inspired
the mightiest efforts of the greatest musical
genius who, as yet, has appeared upon the
scene.

She herself has said of the Zurich period:
" Out of it sprang ' Tristan und Isolde.' The
rest is silence and bowing one's head in rev-
erence." Yes—before Tristan, but no less
before his Isolde.

In 1872 the Wesendonks left Zurich and
settled first in Dresden, later in Berlin.
Their country seat on the Traunsee was pur-
chased in 1878. Wagner sent them the
scores of " Die Meistersinger," " Siegfried,"

and Götterdämmerung," with inscriptions testifying to his feelings of friendship and gratitude. When Siegfried Wagner was studying in Berlin he was a welcome guest at the Wesendonk house. Otto died in 1896, Mathilde, August 31, 1902, in the Traunsee villa after an illness of only a few hours. It was during the last years of her life that she harked back to the romance of which she was the heroine and the greatest of musical geniuses the hero, and prepared the correspondence for publication. She well knew that it only needed to be read to place in its proper light a relation which even in her later years had furnished occasion for malicious comment. The Wagner estate, which had a proprietary interest in the letters, consented to forego its rights, and the correspondence was issued for the benefit of the Bayreuth fund.

In the book are a few letters from Mathilde to Wagner, none later than 1865. Intellectually they are not remarkable, but they show a tender concern and gentle sympathy for his misfortunes. I will quote three characteristic extracts:

THE FABRIC OF DREAMS

" A SILENT CHRISTMAS JOY "
December 25, 1861.

A silent Christmas joy to which I had intended to treat myself, you have brought to nought. On my birthday you were to have received a letter—it is lying in Vienna. On Christmas you were to have been surprised with a little box of trifles in various ways associated with our companionship. The task of gathering them was a joy to me, and I accomplished it with uncommon celerity and ease, secretly fearing that I might be too late. Doubtless the box soon will be returned to me from Vienna.

" THE OLD LONGING "

January 16, 1862.

I have just been reading Schopenhauer's biography, and feel myself indescribably attracted by his character, which seems to have so much in common with yourself. The old longing came over me to gaze again into those beautifully inspired eyes, into the deep mirror of nature that is akin to genius. I thought much of our companionship. The rich world that you spread out before my child-like mind lay before me. My eyes rested with ecstasy on the magic structure. Faster and faster my heart beat with deep gratitude, and I felt that nothing of this would ever be lost to me. So long as I breathe I will strive, and that I owe to you.[1]

"FOR I GLADLY SUFFER WITH YOU"

Schwalbach, August 9, 1863.

Your sad letter sank heavily into my heart. Yet I do not protest against the grief you have caused me by writing thus. For I gladly suffer with you. My whole being feels ennobled in being permitted to share your grief. However sadly the letters stare at me up from the paper, when I ask their meaning, they take on a dear, familiar aspect when I say to myself, " They were written by him for you alone!"

This last letter would form a fitting ending to this story of Wagner and his Isolde. But there is an ending even more appropriate—

1 Besides poems, Mathilde wrote several dramas, ("Gudrun," "Edith, or the Battle of Hastings," "Frederick the Great") fairy tales, puppet plays, and legendary stories. Doubtless Wagner gave her the initial stimulus to literary work.

THE FABRIC OF DREAMS

that poem which Mathilde sent to him and
in which he discovered the musical soul, the
Eternal Feminine, of " Tristan und Isolde ":

"DREAMS"

Tell me what these dreams of wonder
Round my soul their magic weaving,
Not like bubbles, burst asunder,
Naught but void behind them leaving?

Visions, every hour bringing
Heaven's message near and nearer,
Blossoms, from a heart upspringing,
Radiance shedding ever clearer.

Visions ever wider ranging,
Glorious as a sun ne'er setting,
Ecstasy complete, unchanging,
All-remembering, all-forgetting!

Visions like the voices calling
In the springtime, clear and sweet,
Mind and heart and soul enthralling,
As the newborn day they greet;

And each flower's tender blossom,
While exhaling fragrant breath,
Like a twilight in thy bosom,
Fades to silent, rapturous death!

For EU product safety concerns, contact us at Calle de José Abascal, 56–1°,
28003 Madrid, Spain or eugpsr@cambridge.org.

www.ingramcontent.com/pod-product-compliance
Ingram Content Group UK Ltd.
Pitfield, Milton Keynes, MK11 3LW, UK
UKHW040617240426
470322UK00010B/166

* 9 7 8 1 1 0 8 0 7 8 5 5 9 *